PAGE 1   *Classie Bawn Castle, near Mullaghmore, County Sligo,
one of the residences of the Mountbatten family*

PAGES 2 AND 3   *The Glen of Aherlow, County Tipperary, lies on the
northern side of the Galty Mountains. It was once an important pass between the plains
of Counties Tipperary and Limerick.*

4

ABOVE *Farmhouse near the seaside resort of Lahinch, County Clare*

OPPOSITE, ABOVE *Two French fleets, in 1689 and 1796, attempted the invasion of Ireland by entering Bantry Bay.*

IRISH TRADITIONS

EDITED BY KATHLEEN JO RYAN & BERNARD SHARE

PHOTOGRAPHS BY KATHLEEN JO RYAN

WITH ESSAYS BY CYRIL CUSACK, CAOIMHÍN Ó DANACHAIR, SEAMUS DEANE, BRIAN FALLON, THE KNIGHT OF GLIN, DESMOND GUINNESS, PETER HARBISON, JOHN B. KEANE, JUSTIN KEATING, BENEDICT KIELY, LORD KILLANIN, HUGH LEONARD, BRYAN MACMAHON, CIARÁN MACMATHÚNA, MÁIRE DE PAOR, JAMES PLUNKETT, PATRICK SHAFFREY, AND PETER SOMERVILLE-LARGE

ABRADALE PRESS

HARRY N. ABRAMS, INC., PUBLISHERS

To my parents, John and Edith Ryan, and my sister, Mischel Denise Ryan, for their unconditional love; to my brother, John Michael Ryan, for his guidance and abundant wisdom; to my extended family for their encouragement and support; to Alec Stern for his inspiration; to Mrs. Dempsey for her soul support in Ireland.

SPONSORS

♣ AER LINGUS

FEI LTD.   *John J. Fogarty, New York & Ireland*

P. J. CARROLL & COMPANY, LIMITED   *Ireland*

▟ VERBATIM CORPORATION   *Sunnyvale, California*
VERBATIM LTD.   *Limerick, Ireland*

B. P. and ALMA McDONOUGH, OWNERS
Dromoland Castle & Clare Inn Hotels
New Market on Fergus, County Clare, Ireland

THE SHAMROCK GROUP
Richard K. Barry
San Francisco, California & Ireland

CONTRIBUTORS

THE AMERICAN IRISH FOUNDATION • JANET & JACK O'LOUGHLIN

JOHN JAMESON IRISH WHISKEY • DIGITAL EQUIPMENT IRELAND

EASTMAN KODAK COMPANY • KODAK IRELAND LIMITED

TROSTAN GROUP LIMITED • JURYS HOTEL GROUP, LTD.

VIVIAN McATEER • OWEN STEBBINS • DECLAN COLLINS

MISCHEL DENISE RYAN • CHRIS & FRAN STRITZINGER

CAROL TAYLOR • ROBERT T. NAHAS

The generous support of the sponsors and contributors listed above made *Irish Traditions* possible. This is an opportunity to thank each publicly for their vision in seeing the potential of the dream and committing themselves to its success.
Here is a big thank you to all.

CONTENTS

CONTENTS

INTRODUCTION

JAMES PLUNKETT

In the year 1898 W. B. Yeats and Edward Martyn traveled specially to see the writer George Moore in London to beg him to return to Ireland to help them to set up their new Drama Movement; Martyn, in his enthusiasm, assured him that 1899 was going to be the beginning of a Celtic Renaissance. Moore was dismissive. The Celt, he told them, badly needed a renaissance; he'd been going down the hill for the past two thousand years.

It was a dusty answer for the eager travelers. But Moore, no doubt, had in mind the ravaged landscapes of his own adolescence of the mid-1860s: those ruined abbeys, the shattered crosses, round towers broken off at the top, and the peasant cabins tenantless among the thorns and the nettles. A landlord himself (and a Catholic one into the bargain), he had known those tumbled cabins when they were not only occupied but overcrowded and swarming, with their dung pits in hillocks in front of the doors and the rough stone causeways making a path among the stagnant pools of seepage. What, he may well have asked himself, could such deprivation entomb that could possibly be worth disinterring?

For Moore had already pondered on the debasement of the tenant class and the pitilessness of his own: "Until the 'seventies Ireland was feudal and we looked upon our tenants as animals that lived in hovels round the bogs, whence they came twice a year with their rents. . . . And out of tall hats came rolls of banknotes so dirty that my father grumbled, telling the tenant he must bring cleaner notes. . . . And if they failed to pay their rents, the cabins they had built with their own hands were thrown down, for there was no pity for a man who failed to pay his rent."

Not only had Moore, in his coldly sympathetic way, noted the plight of the tenantry, he had predicted the ruin of the landlords as its necessary outcome and visualized, before it came to pass, the signs of that downfall: the Big Houses tottering behind rusting entrance gates and the walls breached about neglected estates.

Nevertheless, when he came to Dublin (Moore's curiosity always outweighed his prejudices) he soon realized that something quite unusual was indeed under way. Traditional Ireland, which had almost died of neglect, was being rediscovered; there was a new and enthusiastic determination to revive the Irish language; native and foreign scholars were struggling with the obscurities of ancient Gaelic manuscripts and their translations were appearing regularly. The oral art of the old-time storyteller was being transcribed; poets and writers were turning to these rich and untapped sources of native myth and folklore for inspiration. The dung pits, it was being discovered, had had more behind them than an inert and derisory subrace. In the souls beneath the animal forms so beloved of the British cartoonists (the shillelagh, the claw-hammer coat, the piglike nostrils, sagging chin, and overhanging lip) there glimmered, like a tiny candle in some deep-buried dungeon, the unquenchable gift of Apprehension.

So Moore, becoming part and parcel of the excitement and the resurgence, wrote as his own contribution a book of short stories called *The Untilled Field*, which reflected the daily round of existence among the ordinary people of his native County Mayo. He had it translated into Irish to serve (as he put it) as a technical model for the new and inexperienced writers who were expected to begin creating a modern literature in the native tongue. In the event, the book was largely ignored by the Gaelic-language enthusiasts, possibly because the eye Moore cast over peasant life was too unsentimental and unromantic. Nevertheless, the English version remains a powerfully original and faithful portrayal of rural life at the end of the nineteenth century.

The poet W. B. Yeats became an indefatigable searcher after that hidden Ireland; on his own, in the cottages of County Sligo and the quayside boats in Sligo Town; with Lady Gregory in the countryside around Coole Park estate (there is a story that he had to give up wearing his poet's all-black outfit because the people mistook him for a priest all the time and kept addressing him as "Father"). J. M. Synge wandered in solitude in Wicklow and Mayo and the Aran Islands, learning Irish and picking up themes for plays about peasant life, some of which shocked the more national- istic and caused riots in the theater when they were staged. But his most remarkable find was not the individual themes but a new and passionate language based on peasant speech. "A certain number of the phrases I employ [he wrote] I have heard from herds- and fishermen along the coast from Kerry to Mayo, or from beggarwomen and ballad singers nearer Dublin. . . . Anyone who has lived in real intimacy with the Irish peasantry will know that the wildest sayings and ideas in this play [*The Playboy of the Western World*] are tame indeed, compared with the fancies one may hear in any little hillside cabin in Geesala or Carraroe, or Dingle Bay."

Others were searching out the common and neglected heritage too, while the Gaelic League teachers made their ways down remote boreens to tutor the townspeople and villagers in the Irish language. The leaders were to become household names: Douglas Hyde, founder of the Gaelic League in 1893 who, in 1937, became the first President of an independent Ireland; Sir Horace Plunkett, who started the cooperative movement in agriculture; Arthur Griffith, the architect of Sinn Féin (ourselves alone); and Yeats and Martyn, Lady Gregory and J. M. Synge, who set up the National Theatre. The "Terrible Beauty" that Yeats wrote about was being born.

At this time, of course, Ireland was still territorially undivided and consisted of all thirty-two counties, so that the reawakened concern about the sagas and legends of Irish mythology, about Gaelic literature, about folklore, folkways, and folk beliefs, found expression among all creeds and classes throughout the whole of the country. It was a reawakening that ranged from culture and language to affectionate re-evaluation of the humble garniture of everyday street life. St. John Ervine, the Belfast playwright, who was a manager of the Abbey Theatre, continued over long years to supply it with plays depicting Northern character and Northern life, and in later years poets such as Louis MacNeice and W. R. Rodgers contributed consistently and copiously to the regeneration of a distinctive style in Irish poetry. Perhaps the most persistent in declaring both his Planter origins and his right to be Irish has been the poet John Hewitt, who laid it all on the line when he wrote:

> This is our country also—nowhere else
> And we shall not be outcast on the world.

In such bodies as the Ulster Folk Museum the traditional crafts and architecture are protected and preserved, while in a recent book by Alice Kane the songs and sayings of an Ulster childhood have been painstakingly recorded and perpetuated.

There were, of course, disagreements from time to time as to what was, and was not, truly Irish and genuinely rooted in custom. In my own childhood, we children of Dublin city found ourselves often enough at loggerheads with our schoolteachers on this particular question. For the most part they came from rural backgrounds and their notion of what constituted "Irishness" bore little relationship to the realities of the Dublin experience. Gaelic football, traditional music, and the Irish language had been natural to their world. They were remote from ours, as remote as thatched cottages or turf fires. On the other hand, our passion for soccer football, especially Cross-Channel football, drew stern disapproval. Soccer, we were told, was a garrison game and following it, never mind playing it, was an abandonment of our national heritage.

There were other unexpected manifestations of a romantic nationalism that at times could get out of proportion. Daniel O'Connell (1775–1847), honored by history with the title "the Liberator" because of his success in winning Catholic Emancipation in 1829, was now frowned upon, on the grounds that he had once freely declared his conviction that the saving of a country, by which he meant the saving of Ireland, was not worth the shedding of a single drop of blood. Dan was a constitutionalist and his pacifist sentiment was rejected by a romantic nationalism of the more sinister kind, which in due course became neither romantic nor nationalist but terrorist and internationalist.

Less ominous, though equally ludicrous, was the rejection of Tom Moore, whose *Moore's Melodies*, first published in 1807, made his name known in every homestead in the country and gained for him the title of Ireland's National Poet. The complaint was that Tom's singing had won equal success and approval in the early-nineteenth-century drawing rooms of the British aristocracy. This came to be regarded as a black mark against him and, although it did little to diminish his popularity, it demonstrated a failure to grasp the fact that to the artist the beliefs and customs and traditions that go to make up the often contradictory elements of an accumulated culture are welded by the passage of time into an indivisible whole.

If we often had to agree to disagree on such matters, there was a considerable area in which custom and tradition differed not at all. Certain practices and beliefs prevailed everywhere. On the eve of All Souls' Day, for instance, my mother, in common with mothers all across the country, would leave a bowl of water on the kitchen table before going to bed. It was her belief that on All Souls' Eve, the souls in purgatory enjoyed the privilege of being released from midnight until dawn and the bowl of water was to slake their thirst. Similarly, on Christmas Eve she would set a lighted candle in the window to guide the Holy Family who, it was believed, walked the roads of Ireland on that night seeking shelter. And on the stroke of three on Good Friday she would drop whatever she was doing and sit or kneel in silence because that was when the crucified Christ had died.

We youngsters had our own customs and practices. One peculiar one was to spit out if we passed a dead animal of any kind, the belief being that the soul of the rat or the dog or whatever it happened to be would be looking for a new body to inhabit and might well try to slip in through your mouth. It was a procedure that probably related back to an ancient belief in the transmigration of souls. In the same way we said "God Bless You" if a companion sneezed, again in the belief that a spirit had tried to make a furtive entry. We also honored the rituals of Hallowe'en: the games, the use of earth and ashes to divine the future. We dressed up and wandered the streets and knocked on doors requesting token gifts of fruit or money.

As for music and the Irish language, I now remember that, of course, my maternal grandfather supplied both. He was a carpenter by trade and used to make fiddles, which he would play sitting at the fireside in his high wooden armchair, his pipe rack visible behind his right shoulder and, as like as not, his bowler hat perched forgotten on his head. The Irish he spoke was Donegal Irish and whenever he lapsed into it, it displeased my grandmother, who considered it an ill-bred habit and regressive.

Those were things of childhood. The most memorable brush with the heritage of history came as a young man in the company of Frank O'Connor. Apart from his short stories, Frank became a most accomplished translator of Irish poetry, but especially the poetry that had emanated from the early Irish monastic movement. And he collected ancient monasteries the way others collect stamps. During one memorable summer he took me around over a period of a fortnight during which we visited—among many other sites—Clonmacnoise, Cashel, Jerpoint, Holy Cross, and the island monasteries of Inish Cleraun and Inis Cealtra. At Clonmacnoise one looked at the width of the Shannon as it flowed by and thought with wonder that over a thousand years ago it was a broad highway for the coracles of the missionary monks.

Jerpoint was a cause for wonder of a different kind. We mounted a tower and I saw Frank's eyes lighting up as he scanned his surroundings: "Ah," he said, in a voice that vibrated with satisfaction: "Chaucer country."

This book is a pictorial essay on the subject of the native heritage, an interpretation of the landscape through a series of superbly studied photographs. It reminds one that George Bernard Shaw was overwhelmed by the transfiguration of Dublin city and the encircling mountains as the morning light billowed landward from the sea about Killiney. And Oliver St. John Gogarty, too, was obliged to halt his walk on Sandymount Strand to marvel at the sudden transformation of shape and color above the hill of Howth. But, having begun with George Moore, perhaps it is as well to end with him and his description of the shores of Lough Carra on the day his mother died: "My mother died certainly on the most beautiful day I had ever seen, the most winsome, the most white, the most wanton, as full of love as a girl in a lane who stops to gather a spray of hawthorn. How many times, like many another, did I wonder why death should have come to anyone on such a bridal-like day."

Evocation? Apprehension? Let us leave it at that.

PAGE 17 *Saint Kevin's Cross, Glendalough, County Wicklow*

ABOVE *The Hill of Tara was the seat of the kings and high kings of Ireland from the Bronze Age to* A.D. *1022. It is situated in County Meath, some thirty miles from Dublin.*

OPPOSITE *Tara. A statue of Saint Patrick, erected about a hundred years ago*

PAGES 20 AND 21 *Prehistoric stone circle, West Cork.*
The provenance of these monuments is uncertain.

ABOVE *Bronze Age stone circles, Beaghmore, County Tyrone. This recently*
discovered group includes seven circles, nine alignments, and twelve cairns.

OPPOSITE, ABOVE *Poulnabrone portal dolmen, County Clare, dates from*
about 3000 B.C. The capstone measures twelve feet by seven feet.

OPPOSITE, BELOW *Haroldstown Dolmen, County Carlow*

The monastic settlement on the Skellig Islands, off the coast of County Kerry, was founded in the sixth century. A view from Great Skellig, or Sceiligh Micheál

Dunluce Castle, County Antrim, built about 1300 by Richard de Burgh,
Earl of Ulster. In 1639 part of the kitchen with eight servants sank into a cave during a storm.

PAGE 26 *The round tower, Glendalough, is still virtually perfect after 1000 years.*

PAGE 27 *The round tower at Kilmacduagh, County Galway. Over a
hundred feet high, it leans slightly out of the perpendicular.*

ABOVE *The Rock of Cashel, County Tipperary, was the seat of the Munster kings,
and it is particularly identified with King Brian Boru (926–1014).*

OPPOSITE *Cormac's Chapel, Cashel, County Tipperary, built between 1127
and 1134 by Cormac McCarthy, King of Desmond and Bishop of Cashel*

28

ABOVE *Prehistoric ring forts are a common feature of the countryside. Few have been excavated, and they are, or were, popularly identified as residences of ''the little people.''*

LEFT *Bog cotton is a common sight on turf bogs in all parts of the country.*

OPPOSITE *Barley Cove, West Cork. The swan figures prominently in Celtic legend.*

PAGE 32 *The Burren, County Clare: traditional rural architecture with half-door*

DESCENDED FROM GODS, KINGS, AND HEROES

BY MÁIRE DE PAOR

Like most ancient peoples, the Irish had many origin legends, telling how they were descended from gods, kings, and heroes. With the coming of Christianity and literacy, they became acquainted with great structured chronicles, such as the Bible, and they set about writing their own synthetic history of origins, embodying the legends. *Lebor Gabála Erenn* ("Book of the Takings of Ireland") recounts the fabulous history of all the successive peoples who occupied the land and is full of colorful stories drawn from Ireland's ancient Celtic mythology.

Five peoples are named as taking Ireland before the Gael, ending with the Tuatha Dé Danann, whose coming is described: "Thus did they come in dark clouds. They landed on the mountains of Conmaicne Réin in Connachta and they cast a darkness upon the sun for three days and three nights. They demanded battle or kingship of the Fir Bolg [the previous invaders]. A battle was fought between them, namely the first battle of Magh Tuired, in which there fell one hundred thousand of the Fir Bolg. After that they took the kingship of Ireland." It is clear that the Tuatha Dé were the gods of the Celts, and their mythological nature was disguised when the origin legends were written down in Christian times. The location of the battle at Magh Tuired is of more interest when we wish to move from myth to actuality, for this district in County Sligo contains a great many megalithic monuments, obviously built by settlers who were there before the Celts.

And it is to archaeology that we must turn to find out something of the early peoples of Ireland. The basic genetic stock was probably a Mesolithic, or Middle Stone Age, people who arrived by way of northern Britain about 7000 B.C., soon after the end of the Ice

Age. They brought with them a tradition of fishing and food gathering. No monuments survive from this time, but we have found tools of flint and bone and food refuse by rivers and the seashore in the North and East of the country. This way of life lasted for a long time, and the culture has close affinities with those of British and Continental forest and coastal dwellers. Gradually (between 4000 and 2000 B.C.) groups of Neolithic immigrants arrived. They came from the general direction of France and Spain, and some of them had North African origins. They brought a knowledge of agriculture and have left a striking testament in the form of the great megalithic tombs still to be seen throughout the country. We can begin to know something of the mind, religious beliefs, and social organization of people who erected such monuments as Newgrange and Knowth in County Meath or Carrowkeel and Creevykeel in County Sligo. Mesolithic people seem to have survived and mingled with the newcomers.

More groups of immigrants are indicated by the arrival of a knowledge of bronze-working about 2000 B.C., and from then on new fashions in tools, ornaments, weapons, and funeral rites display constant intercourse, probably including migration, between Ireland and Britain and parts of the Continent. In the Late Bronze Age, about 700 B.C., there are strong Scandinavian, Iberian, and British connections. The best analogy is probably with the stockpot, where the soup is added to from time to time. There is never the same mix of people in any two centuries.

We are not sure exactly when Celtic-speaking people arrived (sometime in the last millennium B.C.), nor do we know how large the immigrations need have been to achieve the gradual imposition of the Irish language. It is possible that quite a small number of people were involved, but they became dominant through the aristocratic prestige of their victorious warriors. Weapons and ornaments with the elegant, curvilinear abstract forms of La Tène (Continental) Celtic art are known in Ireland from about the third century B.C. Traces of older non-Indo–European languages survive in Irish, possibly, as Heinrich Wagner has suggested, of North African origin. And as Caoimhín Ó Danachair has pointed out, the Irish calendar is solar, not lunar, and probably also reflects pre-Celtic traditions. Certainly by the time of Christ Gaelic speech was dominant, and although Ireland was not yet literate, place names and tribal names are known from Greek and Latin sources. With the coming of Christianity and literacy, we can begin to say much more about the people of Ireland, the structure of their society, and their way of life.

Ethnically they were very mixed, but when Irish history really begins in the fifth century A.D., all the earlier peoples had been completely Celticized and they shared a common language and a common culture. The early sagas were not written down until the seventh or eighth century and are preserved in still later manuscripts, but they incorporate much oral tradition of earlier times and give a vivid picture of society. We can recognize many of the same features that are depicted in Greek accounts of the Continental Celts—a warlike, aristocratic society with an economy based on agriculture. Many archaic features of Celtic life were preserved in Ireland long after they had disappeared on the Continent and indeed lasted up until the Norman invasion in the twelfth century. Kingship, an ancient Indo–European institution, survived. The king, besides being a ruler, was a sacred person descended from the ancestral god of his tribe. He entered on his rule by taking part in inauguration rites whereby he became the embodiment of his people, wedded to the soil. The country is a woman, the spouse the king, and when the rightful king reigns, the land is fertile and free from natural misfortunes such as plague or blight. The king was inaugurated at a sacred site, often a prehistoric burial mound, and poets took part in the ceremony.

There were many minor kings, each ruling over a *tuath*, or tribe, on its ancestral lands and paying tribute to an over-king, who ruled the province. By the coming of Christianity the principal over-kings ruled from Tara, in County Meath, and Cashel, in County Tipperary. There was no central government, but Tara remained a symbol of sovereignty long after it had been abandoned as a royal residence. A remarkable group of earthworks—grass-grown ring forts and mounds—still survives at Tara, and before the coming of Christianity this was undoubtedly an important religious site. The presence there of a megalithic tomb that has been excavated and that dates to about 2500 B.C. illustrates the common adoption of pre-Celtic sacred sites by the later Celtic settlers.

Society was rigidly stratified and the different grades are described in the law tracts. There were three main social classes: the landowning aristocracy, or warrior class; the free men, who were also landowners; and the unfree—slaves, laborers, and lower grades of entertainers. But there was another special class, the *aes dána*, men of art, or the learned class, which was equated in rank with the nobility, as the clergy were in Christian times. The *aes dána* included lawyers, poets, historians, and musicians, as well as skilled crafts-men and physicians. They had special privileges and were protected, by legal custom, beyond their own *tuath* and had greater freedom of movement than any other class. The basic and important unit of society was the *fine*, or joint family, and a man's rights and duties were bound up with his membership in various kin groups. Ownership of land was invested in the *fine*, and the *fine* was responsible for the misdeeds of its members. Similarly, each member of a king's family in the male line up to four generations could succeed to the kingship. Direct succession was rare—a cause of many dynastic quarrels. Polygamy, concubinage, and divorce were essential features of dynastic life and were never successfully wiped out by the Church. The numerous Irish genealogical tracts show how important it was to preserve one's family tree. An overweening interest in family relationships has survived in Ireland to the present day.

If we want to know what the people looked like, the anatomist can tell us from the archaeological evidence that they were little different from the present population. The literature tells us that the ideal of beauty, in both pre-Christian and Christian times, was fair skin, golden hair, and blue eyes. Descriptions abound: "The colour of her hair was like the flower of the iris in Summer or like pure gold after it has been polished. She was undoing her hair to wash it so that her arms were out from beneath her dress. White as the snow of one night were her hands, and her lovely cheeks were soft and even, red as the mountain fox-glove. Her eyebrows were as black as a beetle's back. Her teeth were like a shower of pearls. Her eyes were as blue as the hyacinth, her lips as red as Parthian leather. . . ."

This may have been the ideal, but in a population of mixed blood there must have been many physical types. In a twelfth-century text a man advises his son on the choice of a wife: " 'Do not wed the slender short girl with curling hair; nor the stumpy stout girl; nor the weakly tall one; nor the black-haired, ungovernable girl; nor the fair boisterous one; nor the slender, prolific, lascivious girl; nor the ill-spoken one of evil counsels.' 'What girl am I to wed?' 'If you can find them, the fair-haired, broad-shaped ones, the pale-hued black-headed ones.' "

The stylized abstract art is little help in the matter of appearance, although some carvings, as on the doorways at Dysert O'Dea and Clonfert, have elements of portraiture. But in the matter of dress, representations on crosses and in manuscripts support the literary accounts. Dress seems to have been related to social status and is prescribed in the laws. The dress of the aristocracy in pagan Celtic and Christian times consisted of two main garments: the *léine*, or tunic, usually of linen, which could be knee-length, calf-length or ankle-length, and the *brat*, or cloak, made of wool and fastened by a brooch or pin. The *léine* was most often made of unbleached linen but the love of bright color was reflected in the *brat*, which could be purple, crimson, green, yellow, gray, striped, checkered, or black. Men, women, and children wore the same type of dress, and it seems to have varied little right up to the Norman invasion. Trousers may have been worn by some of the lower orders, but they are never mentioned in the texts. Personal ornament was equally prized in pagan and Christian times, and the gold, bronze, and enameled ornaments preserved from Iron Age and Christian times show a love of display and color.

Life was simple and rural. There were no towns until the port cities were founded by the Vikings in the ninth century, and the economy was largely based on cattle. There was no currency, and the basic units of value were the cow and the *cumal* (originally "bondswoman"), who was worth four cows. Milk, butter, cheese, and cream were the main summer food; beef and porridge were winter food. Cattle, too, accounted for most of the wars between *tuath* and *tuath* and province and province. Most battles took the form of raids to drive off enemies' livestock, while the tribute paid by a sub-king to an over-king was largely in the form of cattle. Well-to-do farmers and ranchers did not live in villages but in isolated farmsteads defended by a ditch-and-bank system, which encircled the dwelling house and the outhouses. The remains of thousands of these homesteads can be seen all over Ireland. In the midlands the enclosures were of wood and earth, while in the West they were built of dry stone. Assemblies were a feature of Celtic life, and often the royal sites, the headquarters of the provincial kings—Tara, Cruachan, Aileach, Emain Macha—are marked by more substantial earthworks and citadels of stone.

Feasting, music, poetry, and storytelling were the favorite indoor pastimes; hunting was the favorite outdoor pursuit. The *file*, or poet, retained many of the attributes of the pagan druid, and his satire was greatly feared. His main function originally was to be an apologist for the aristocratic society, but with the coming of Christianity and literacy a new syllabic, lyric poetry came into being, based on Latin hymn meters. As well as the more monotonous official verse there are remarkable nature poems, poems of exile, and personal poems both within and without the monastic tradition. One example must suffice:

> My tidings for you: the stag bells
> Winter snows, summer is gone.
> Wind high and cold, low the sun.
> Short his course, sea running high.
>
> Deep-red the bracken, its shape all gone,
> The wild-goose has raised his wonted cry.
> Cold has caught the wings of birds;
> Season of ice—these are my tidings.*

The characteristics of the people as revealed in the early literature are varied, but some stand out: headstrong pride, generosity, quarrelsomeness, impetuosity, love of nature, and a powerful sense of kinship and family. Generosity and hospitality were greatly valued but also necessary: Together with pride of family they follow from the social system and the aristocratic concept of society. Love of intricacy of pattern in thought, in literature, and in art seems to have been a particularly Irish trait, and one which seems to have survived—as, for example, in the work of James Joyce—despite the later additions of Vikings, Normans, and Britons to the Irish potpourri. Joyce seems to have recognized his kinship with the Celtic tradition, since the Book of Kells is one of the minor obsessive themes of *Finnegans Wake*. Pre-Norman Ireland lacked the ordinary appendages of civilization —coinage, cities, institutions—but it was a civilization in another sense, with its own identity, life, and a unified culture that produced a remarkable literature and a remarkable art.

*Kuno Meyer, *Four Songs of Summer and Winter*. London: 1903, p. 14.

THE IDEAL THEATER OF PLAYWRIGHT AND PLAYER

BY CYRIL CUSACK

R eaction to theater must be, for everyone, personal; and, as an actor, I must cast less than a cold academic eye over the changing stages of Irish theater. So, if you will, I shall take a view from the "wings," as it were, looking in—and back. With me, let us look for beginnings.

I first recite the common litany of Irish playwrights: Farquhar, Congreve, Goldsmith, Sheridan, Kelly, O'Keefe, Murphy, and so on, who, in satire and in the comedy of manners, laid siege to the social climate of their time, rendered by a galaxy of actors from Ireland: Macklin, Spranger, Barry, Ross, Dexter, Mossop, and, of course, that lady so formidable in the "breeches parts," Peg Woffington. Nearer to our time, London's cherished conventions suffered the exquisite shock of Oscar Fingal O'Flahertie Wilde with *The Importance of Being Earnest*, *Lady Windermere's Fan*, and the rest, followed by the pugilism and pyrotechnics of George Bernard Shaw. "But," you ask, "is there a Gaelic theater?"

With memory of uncertain productions of Molière and Ostrovsky in Gaelic, I answer, well, yes, it did emerge, through the early 1930s, though mostly in translation. I have myself directed for the Comhar Drámaíochta, a company of players, dedicated amateurs in the true sense, presenting on the minuscule stage of the Peacock Theatre that very quality of native presence—a unique combination of power and innocence—that made so special the company that W. G. Fay (cofounder with the poet Yeats of the Abbey Theatre) brought to London in 1903, enrapturing English critics. I sing dumb on the doleful disappearance of these gifted actors; but with the amalgamation of the Comhar and the Abbey, the Gaelic theater movement sank into pantomimic echoes of Gaelic myth.

I swing a flashlight around my brain, desperately seeking illumination on the Gaelic scene. A flicker of recollection: Macklin, a Northern Gael who, having mastered the English language, hammered the current attitudinizing into a naturalistic style of acting that came to be the continuing Irish contribution to the stage. Macklin—or McLaughlin—crashed into mid-eighteenth-century London with a revolutionary rendering of Shylock in *The Merchant of Venice*.

A spurt into the present century brings me to dwell, maybe a little too smugly, on that Abbey trio of genius—Synge, Lady Gregory, and Yeats—and their inspired fabrication from Gaelic into English of a new theatrical idiom. What next? Robert Flaherty's classic film documentary, with Gaelic-speaking actors, of life in the Western Isles, *Man of Aran*; then, recently, *Poitín*, a strange story beautifully pictured, again with Gaelic actors, and robed in a darkening atmosphere reminiscent of Maupassant. Ah, yes, but films!

Suddenly, I have it—a brand-new theory—or is it? The origins of Irish theater, of the Irish actor. Surely nobody has thought of it before! For, of course, there is the tradition of the hearth-side recital, drama acted out by the kitchen storyteller, the heroic myth dating from pre-Christian times and relayed through the generations up to the present day. "Cottage theater," I might call it. It might well be that from this has come continuity all the way into modern Irish theater, in the evolution of an Irish acting presence on the stage and in play content—as in Yeats's Cuchulainn cycle and materials drawn from the deeps of Irish mythology by other playwrights (a *Deirdre* from A.E. [George Russell], as well as from Synge; *Deirdre* from Donagh MacDonagh; *Maeve*, Edward Martyn's play at Dublin's Gaiety Theatre in 1900; and George Moore's *The Last Feast of the Fianna*).

Almost as a cliché it has come to us, that combination of playwright and player that is parcel and part of ideal theater. But there are times when the part drifts from the parcel or the parcel rejects the part. Drama may present the conventional features of tragedy and comedy, but often these will make faces, one perhaps the high-and-mighty literary expression, another, only engaging popularity and audience appeal. The poet/playwright of the Abbey placed priority on the spoken word but often failed to give proper recognition to the interior poetry of natural movement and gesture, to the emotive value of pause, and, more important, of silence—to what I term the "interiority" of creative acting.

As to the mythical drama acted out by the hearthstone, that theater ancestry I suggest: I came upon one such storyteller—Peig Sayers.

Fifty years ago, in Dunquin on the mainland, I sat enraptured in her cottage, an audience of one save for the poet son, with nods and smiles, squatting by the hearth. Peig had left her Blasket Islands home, her island washed by the wild Atlantic, like a banshee tearing tousle-haired around its lonely shore. A statuesque presence, almost a transfiguration, she stood high in her kitchen, delivering in mellifluous Gaelic the ancient saga. There you had the Irish stage presence, the pure origin of Gaelic theater.

It is a hurried leap from the myth and mystery of hearth-side histrionics onto the professional stage. Yet, with passing applause for the far-off shuttle of eighteenth-century Irish actors between Dublin's Crow Street and Smock Alley theaters and London's Covent Garden and Drury Lane, one could imagine the grand manner of this cottage drama storming through a curtain of blue turf smoke into a lamplit barn and booth of touring theater; imagine also a parallel movement of audience from kitchen stool to the rough benches of village hall, disused church or courthouse, even boathouse! (In 1919 a boathouse was our theater in Cappoquin, County Waterford.)

It is easy to imagine the heroics merging into the simple patriotic drama of the "fit-ups." The "fit-up" theater, as it was called, obliged the actors themselves to build the stage, sometimes with planks laid across beer barrels, with oil lamps borrowed locally for footlights. I remember a score of such companies fanning out through the country: O'Brien and Ireland's Company, Ira Allan's, Brefni O'Rorke's, the McEntees, Dobell's, Mark Wynn's, the Carrickfords, to name just some. The plays—given some permanent recollection in the paintings of Jack B. Yeats, with titles like *The Boys of Wexford*, *Vinegar Hill*, *Knocknagow* (or *The Homes of Tipperary*), *Pike O'Callaghan*—had as their central characters such historic figures as Patrick Sarsfield, Wolfe Tone, Robert Emmet, Henry Joy McCracken, the country's national heroes. For actors and audience alike there was then full involvement, which included myself, a child actor—in those days an essential ingredient of theater.

The Dion Boucicault repertoire, with its spicing of comedy, found most appeal with those early audiences, in particular *The Colleen Bawn*, *Arrah-na-Pogue*, and *Con the Shaughraun*, of the huge number of plays that poured from that actor/playwright's pen. It must be said also that, with its buoyant stress on the principles of justice and chivalry, this kind of theater served to preserve and foster a spirit of nationalism in the people.

But with a slowly rising tide of national self-consciousness and the emergence of the Irish Literary Renaissance came new sensitivities, and the opprobrious term "stage-Irishman" was coined for common currency. Eventually, touring melodrama faded, to be replaced by an ambitious amateur theater movement, now reaching toward professionalism.

Nevertheless, it must be remembered that, on the professional level, many of Ireland's leading actors, before moving across the Liffey to achieve international fame with the Abbey Theatre, already owed some of their schooling and grooming to Dublin's home of melodrama, the Queen's Royal Theatre. These actors brought with them melodrama's special heritage, that technique once common to all stages, without which, in some awareness, the actor's art can sink into vapid behaviorism.

In a sense, the melodrama has since been repatriated with returning affection and popularity, beginning with Hugh Hunt's production of *The Shaughraun* at the Abbey in 1967 which, the following year, became the highlight of London's International Theatre Festival. Thenceforward, with subsequent Abbey productions, of *Arrah-na-Pogue* and, in Gaelic, *The Colleen Bawn*, came renewed popularity for this "old-grinding-young" type of drama and, from intellectual quarters, patronizing approval of a place for Boucicault in the hierarchy of Irish playwrights. From Boucicault was generated a stage tradition not unfamiliar in the great Sean O'Casey *oeuvre*, not unwelcome even in the didactic drama of Shaw: It is apparent in *The Devil's Disciple* and in the dialogue of *John Bull's Other Island*. And Synge's enjoyment of a Queen's Theatre production of *The Shaughraun* in 1904 is reflected in *The Playboy of the Western World*, while in modern Irish theater the love potions of Boucicault's melodrama find an echo in Brian Friel's internationally acknowledged *Translations*.

Finally, from the early tutelage of the Fay brothers, the highest concentration of Irish theater burst into the present century—with the Abbey's contribution—in a monumental output and quality of playwriting, unique in theater history; there was a steady continuity of plays in frequent flights of genius and rarely below true standards of entertainment.

The Abbey, in its evolution for close to a century, has rocked and gamboled through a maddening variety of motions and emotions, interlacing, interpenetrating, merging and dissevering, but with a repertoire never hardening to perish in mere category. Polonius describing the Players to Hamlet might have been giving us the history of the Abbey Theatre; the poetic drama—the Cuchulainn cycle reaching beyond earthly limits—of Yeats; the pastoral-comical-historical drama of Lady Gregory; the tragical-comical-pastoral extravaganza of Synge (once mistakenly understood for realism by audiences both at home and in America and giving rise to protest and riot); the poetical-comical-tragical urban character creations of O'Casey; then, with no denial of social comment and the flavor of irony, the rural comedy charm of Robinson and Shiels; and so on up to the moderns, the magical medleys of Friel and Tom Murphy, and the parochial-comical-tragical theater of Hugh Leonard paradoxically answering a universal thirst at our parish pump—all in full consent and command of acting styles ranging from flamboyance to easy naturalism.

The tale of riot and ructions has been fully told. There were, of course, "incidents," some that cling to my memory: Yeats, from the stage of the Abbey Theatre, pontifically announcing on the first night of *Purgatory* that here was to be found his total philosophy; Yeats—always Yeats!—rejecting O'Casey for *The Silver Tassie*; O'Casey rejecting Yeats for Yeats; again Yeats, hardly blessed with the common touch of humor, huffily quitting the theater because of a Shiels play, *Cartney and Kevney*; Barry Fitzgerald, the Abbey's classic comedian, relegated to a mere "walk-on" part in *Parnell of Avondale*, thus cueing his deliberate exit to America; then, during rehearsals of a Sean O'Faolain play, *She Had to Do Something*, a second company's "sit-in" strike over the replacement of an Irish professional actress by an amateur from abroad; suspension as musical director for composer Frederick May, for organizing without authority a performance of *Quin's Secret*—to take place in the home of its invalid author, Shiels! These, no more no less than family fracases, in the end only served to weld the Abbey into the vital Irish theatrical family that we know.

Emphasis on the purely Irish connection tends naturally toward the National Theatre, which is not to say that there are no other ingredients in the growth of Ireland's theater tradition, others worthy indeed of more than passing mention—the Dublin Drama League;

the Touring McMasters (known provincially as "Mr. and Mrs. Shakespeare," last of the major "fit-up" companies); the Lyric Theatre, vehicle for the playfully satirical playlets of poet Austin Clarke; the Taibhdhearc in Galway; and coming up to the present time, the Pike Theatre, where Brendan Behan's *The Quare Fellow* was first presented; the Focus, a style of Stanislavsky theater; the Project, with a slight turn to the Left; Fieldday Theatre in the North (founded by playwright Friel and poet Seamus Heaney); and now Galway's latest recruit, the Druid Theatre.

However, after the Abbey, the major contribution to theater in Ireland came with the spontaneous emergence of the Dublin Gate Theatre. Billowing and bellowing through the 1930s in the wake of gusty winds from the Continent and our neighbor island, the Gate was set in motion on the turbulent seas of Irish theater, piloted by that remarkable combination of talents, Hilton Edwards, a combative genius, professional to his fingertips and sacrificing not one whit of his Englishness and inheritance of traditional English theatricality, joined with Michael MacLiammoir, Ireland's most romantic actor, who was also a playwright, a designer of distinction, and a fluent Gaelic speaker. Paradoxically, the Gate had its launching from the heart of Gaeldom with MacLiammoir's epic drama based on the mythical story of Diarmuid and Gráinne. It was only a matter of a few years before the Gate, resting, sometimes restlessly, on the pillars of MacLiammoir and Edwards, was built into a theater of account. It attracted a major playwright in Denis Johnston who, topping a stream of plays into the repertoire, made history with *The Old Lady Says No.*

Betweentimes, the Earl of Longford, who later set up his company of Longford Players, took the tiller of this glittering bark; here steering into the mists of Irish history with his amber-lit tale of Swift, *Yahoo*, there toward the myths of ancient Greece with his translation of *Agamemnon*.

MacLiammoir and Edwards brought an embroidery of light and color into the stark decor of Irish theater and this, with the blessing of Yeats, heralded the arrival in the Abbey of Hugh Hunt, a gifted young director from Oxford who, giving his talent, energies, and concern to the Irish National Theatre, together with the internationally known designer Tanya Moiseiwitsch, lifted production to a new level of creativity and effectiveness, since relayed through the directorial talents of MacAnna and Dowling.

I have just read from Hugh Hunt's deeply researched history of the Abbey the following: "Synge, intuitively and by observation, felt that the pre-Christian substratum of the Irish mind was still the most important factor in the conduct of daily life."

So much for my grand "discovery"—the origin and evolution of our Irish theater stemming from country kitchens and bursting into flower with the Abbey. Clearly, the Abbey's early repertoire of a play a week, apparently miraculous, was no simple genesis over seven days and nights. So may it be said in conclusion—and no revelation!—that from the earthly reality of the cottage actor of ancient myth came the molding of our theater and of a constant native presence on the Irish stage.

Inheritors are we all.

THE QUALITY OF NEIGHBORLINESS

BY JOHN B. KEANE

When one considers the traditional scene in rural Ireland the quality that asserts itself is that of neighborliness. It characterized the life-style of the people more than anything else. It was and still is the dominant factor in the social and religious life of every rural parish. The more isolated the region, the more powerful the ties that bind the people together. The great Gaelic poets—Eoghan Ruadh O'Sullivan, Aodhagan O'Rahilly, Geoffrey O'Donoghue, and Pierce Ferriter—praised generosity most of all, repeatedly affirming that it was the greatest of virtues. Generosity is the core of neighborliness. We need only recall the cutting and saving of turf and hay to remind us of what neighborliness means. Neighbor helped neighbor and if the neighbor happened to be a widow or was physically disabled, the help was even more assured.

The rural community was one big family. Everybody knew what everybody else had. The stalks on the potato drills advertised the density of the crop underneath. Cows, calves, and cocks of hay were easily counted from a distance. Hens and chickens were there for all to see. It was easy to guess how much milk was being sent to the creamery, how many eggs were being laid, how many pigs were being killed or taken to market.

Want was as visible as plenty, and rural tradition ordained that the strong come to the aid of the weak, and the well-off to the aid of the poorly-off.

Perhaps nowhere else was the quality of neighborliness so evident in rural Ireland than at "the Stations," the occasions when the priests of the parish visited the house whose turn for the Stations it was, twice a year, said Mass, preached on some relevant topic and afterward mingled with those who came to the "Station Mass." The Stations are still held in many dioceses.

The custom of the Stations is rooted in history. It is generally accepted that it goes back to the Penal days when Mass was outlawed in many rural areas. The Penal Laws consisted of acts passed by successive British governments against Catholics in Ireland from 1537 until Catholic Emancipation in 1829. It was not possible to erect a church, so the priest visited a particular district, said Mass in a home, catechized the children, visited the sick, and administered the sacraments.

There were two other beneficial side effects: the painting and repairing of designated houses (many would have fallen down but for the Stations) and the opportunity given to the local matchmaker to ply his trade. At a Station gathering, eligible spinsters and bachelors were decked out in their Sunday best, but an innate rustic shyness prevented them from speaking for themselves, so they confided in the matchmaker, always an agreeable and articulate fellow.

Matchmaking, once the preserve of the local matchmaker, seems now to be confined to computerization in most areas, although Lisdoonvarna in County Clare has a matchmaking season in September when the resort is crowded, mostly with members of the farming community. There is, in fact, a matchmaker practicing in the hills of West Limerick at the time of this writing. He is Patrick Ahern of Glenshannold, Carrigkerry, and he has over fifty successful marriages to his credit to date.

Unquestionably the greatest matchmaker of all was the late Dan Paddy Andy O'Sullivan of Renagown, Lyreacrompane, in the center of the Stacks Mountains. Dan was responsible for over four hundred marriages. He had only one failure. Dan once told me, in his own inimitable way, that this was due to an inexplicable reluctance on the part of the bride to participate in any form of bed sharing with her husband.

The local matchmaker was a boon to his community. He was sensitive to the mental shortcomings and physical deficiencies of his clients. The song might say that only the brave deserved the fair, but Dan would hold that every old shoe deserved an old stocking. Matchmaking deservedly lives on in the traditional as well as the modern form.

While Irish county people have won renown for their friendliness and hospitality, ranks are quickly closed in the face of overly curious strangers or prying authority, particularly when a friend or neighbor is involved. A member of the Garda Síochána (police force) investigating a serious crime will be well received, invited to partake of the best the house has to offer, but there is surprising stinginess when it comes to the imparting of information. There is a deeply held belief that God will deal in His own way and in His own good time with the transgressor, and that this should be punishment enough. Add to this the fact that the callous and brutal English Penal Law is still fresh in the memory —transportation abroad for life for the poaching of a pheasant, hare, or salmon—and it becomes easier to understand why modern salmon poaching on a massive and destructive scale, resulting in perilously low stocks, is seldom, if ever, reported to the authorities.

Questions relating to petty crimes are deflected rather than left unanswered. A senior detective from Dublin Castle, the police headquarters in Dublin, was questioning a Clare trawlerman about an unsolved crime in the area. The detective pointed to the Aran Islands offshore and asked, "What is the name of the island nearest to us?" To which the Clare man replied, after a long look at the island in question, "Well, would you believe, sir, but I never noticed that island till now."

Then there was the Kerryman who was a witness for the defense in a District Court case. The prosecuting attorney was nearly at his wits' end, having failed hopelessly to elicit a worthwhile answer from his hostile witness all morning. "Tell me," he said sarcastically, "if it's true that a Kerryman will always answer a question with another question?" "Now who in God's name told you that?" said the Kerryman.

These shortcomings aside, the traditional kindness and cordiality of Irish country people was, and is, one of the crowning glories of the Irish nature. In Sigerson Clifford's lovely poem "The Ballad of the Tinker's Wife," the tinker tells his wife-to-be that

> The hall door of the Planter
> Is colder than the East Wind

implying that the Ascendancy classes, once lords and masters of the land, might not take too kindly to tinker folk, although this was not always true. However, in the same poem, the tinker later consoles his promised bride when he boasts that

> The little homes of Kerry
> Will give us half their own

This is still true of most of the small homes of rural Ireland.

One of the most cherished aspects of the rural scene in today's Ireland is that there are still pockets to be found where life is lived almost as it was a generation, and sometimes two or three generations, ago. The ass and cart and the pony and cart are still used for transporting milk from the small dairy farms to the creameries. Elsewhere, giant milk tankers trundle brimful and thunderous over narrow roads, particularly in North Kerry, where the milk cow is the queen of the economy.

Here in the heartland of the cow-filled, fleecy pastures is preserved one of these pockets: the residence of Davy and Mamie Gunn in the townland of Trieneragh, Listowel, County Kerry. Morning and evening, through spring, summer, and autumn, Mamie and Davy hand-milk the five cows that provide a substantial part of their income. Each morning the milk is cooled and transferred to two small aluminum tanks, then loaded on the ass cart, which is driven to the creamery three miles away in Listowel by Mamie. At the creamery she deposits the milk and gleans whatever information is going the rounds. She then ties the ass to a convenient telephone pole and does her shopping.

Meanwhile at home, Davy is preoccupied with the business of *bodhrán*-making. The *bodhrán* is the one-sided goatskin drum beloved of traditional musicians. It was also put to wide and wonderful use by the late and great composer Sean O'Riada, who first saw the *bodhrán* when it was introduced to the Dublin stage at the Abbey Theatre in the summer of 1959 in my play *Sive*, in a production by the Listowel Drama Group.

Davy Gunn, utilizing the same skills and implements used by his father and grandfather, manufactures his much-sought-after *bodhráns* in a tiny workshop attached to his house. First, a suitable goat has to be located, preferably a white female, three to four years old. Experts maintain that the skin of such an animal provides the best sound. Secondly, the goat has to be slaughtered, and this is done painlessly and swiftly with a sharp knife. Then the goat is skinned and the skin is cured. This is a simple process. Lime is spread on the hairy side. The skin is then rolled up tightly and kept thus until all the hair has been burned away by the lime. It is then steeped for a day or two in spring water, then stretched fully and tacked on to a wooden rim. Davy sells his *bodhráns* to musicians and wren-boys.

The wren-boy is so called because of the custom of hunting the wren on the afternoon of Christmas Day. A large number of boys and young men, representing a townland or a parish, would gather at an appointed spot and scour the countryside for the tiny wren. The hunt would be persisted with until the wren was captured, dead or alive. Then on Saint Stephen's Day the wren, if alive, would be borne from house to house in a tiny cage or, if dead, tied to a holly bough. It was a cruel custom but falsely justified by the ancient belief that it was the wren who betrayed Christ to His persecutors before His execution.

The wren-boy's band is still a vital, vibrant part of the Irish traditional folk scene. The custom goes back to early Christian times and was once common to most Celtic countries. Until recent times the wren-boy was a common sight on the Isle of Man and, around the turn of the century, in Cornwall and Brittany. The custom has now died out everywhere except in rural Ireland.

The wren-boys, dressed in peaked caps and white uniforms, crisscrossed with green, red, and yellow sashes, visit all the houses of a specified area from dawn until dark. In return for the money collected, they perform ritual dances and provide traditional music from *bodhrán*, fiddle, melodeon, bones, and concertina. Dancing, singing, and drinking go on until morning lights the winter sky. There is an All-Ireland Wren-boys Bands Championship held in the great square of Listowel, County Kerry, every year on the last Friday in September. Here is seen the finest spectacle of this folk art in rural Ireland, with bands from each of the four provinces competing. A crowd of twenty thousand people assembles in the square to clap and cheer the performing wren-boys.

September meant one thing to Listowel. To seaside places it meant something else. The taking of holidays was hardly part of the traditional scene in rural areas, although the owners of fairly large holdings were not above taking a few weeks' respite in coastal resorts like Ballybunion, Bundoran, Tramore, or Kilkee. They would not dream of holidaying at the aforementioned places during peak periods such as June, July, or August. For one thing, the harvest had to be saved and secondly, with characteristic, rustic modesty, they did not consider themselves good enough. In Ballybunion, Ireland's loveliest seaside resort, there was a name for them. They were known as Buds, and in more recent times as Septobers, because they unfailingly arrived all through September and, depending on the weather, well into October. The Buds were drawn from the strong farming stock of the counties of Cork, Limerick, and Kerry. They never holidayed until the harvest was saved. In fact, it would be unthinkable for them to go away for a weekend at any other time of the year. Ballybunion was their watering place for generations.

The word *Bud* is a corruption of the Irish word *bodaire*, which means a churl, or uncouth person. While they may have seemed churlish at a casual, ignorant glance, they were anything but. They brought with them to Ballybunion a rich, rare, and religious life-style.

I remember them well from the prewar days of the middle and late thirties. As youngsters, we would ape their exaggerated walking styles as they headed for the beach. They mixed only with each other, restricting their walks from lodgings to beach to church, where they prayed several times a day, and finally to bars, where the males indulged moderately. The females waited patiently behind in the Budhouse, or lodging house, for snippets of public-house news.

The Buds brought most of their provisions with them, chiefly eggs, scones, potatoes, vegetables, and home-cured bacon. Each egg was marked with the initials of its proprietor before it was boiled. Also it might be marked *H* for hard, *M* for medium, or *S* for soft. I remember a relation who marked his eggs *S for J.K.*, meaning soft for John Keane, and another who marked his *C.B.* for cannonballs, meaning he wanted them really hard. I remember a local humorous ballad relating to Buds and eggs:

> In came the Ballybunion Buds their vittles for to ate,
> 'Twas hard-boiled eggs and griddle bread and lumps of hairy "mate,"
> 'Twas hard-boiled eggs for breakfast and 'twas hard-boiled eggs for tea,
> You could hear the creatures clucking and they facing for the sea.

In a nook over a mighty Stanley range in the kitchen there was a box that contained several spools of thread, each of a different color. Every slice of bacon was adorned with a particular thread so that the owner could identify it when the bacon was boiled. On Sunday they indulged in fresh meat, generally chops, purchased the previous Saturday from a local butcher. They referred to chops as "mutton rashers."

At night they danced sets, half-sets, and polkas to their own music of fiddle and concertina. They sang ancient songs in English and Irish, and they told old folktales before saying the rosary together and repairing to bed.

Only once would the females bathe, and that was always in the privacy of the caves in the cliffs overlooking the beach where, with lookouts well posted, they would remove their undergarments and submit to the salving sea water that most private area of the anatomy, and you may be certain that it would not have been exposed to the open air since the same period one year before.

After the Second World War, the Buds, as I knew them, disappeared forever. Without fuss, bustle, ostentation, or any other outward display of emotion, they vacated the scene they had cherished for so long. No tear, no lamentation whatsoever, marked their departure. Neither drum nor trumpet was sounded as they faded into the treasury of things past, there to remain till resurrected, maybe by the persistence of folk memory.

There are many songs about the Buds. Here is the final stanza of one that is still sung:

> I walk along a sandy shore beside a silver sea
> Where every wave and ripple there remind me, love, of thee.
> And when at night the stars are bright beside the pale moon's glow,
> I'll dream of Ballybunion and the Buds of long ago.

PAGE 49 *A morning walk near Letterfrack, Connemara, County Galway*

ABOVE *Milking time, The Burren, County Clare*

OPPOSITE *Mamie and Davy Gunn, Listowel, County Kerry. Mamie is ready to leave with the morning delivery of milk to the creamery, Davy to work at his shop, where he makes the* bodhrán, *the traditional goat skin drum.*

ABOVE   *Pony and colt, Connemara Pony Show, Clifden, County Galway*

OPPOSITE, ABOVE   *Assessing the competition, Connemara Pony Show*

OPPOSITE, BELOW LEFT   *Feeding time, Coleraine, County Derry*

OPPOSITE, BELOW RIGHT   *A farm boy accompanies his father
to the creamery at Listowel.*

ABOVE West Cork transportation: The bicycle is still popular in rural areas, and it is making a comeback in the cities.

LEFT Natural resources, Sperrin Mountains, County Tyrone

OPPOSITE, ABOVE A County Down boreen

OPPOSITE, BELOW Near Portrush, County Antrim

PAGE 58, ABOVE *Potato harvest, Kilkeel, County Down*

PAGE 58, BELOW *Winter fuel. Turf (or peat) is Ireland's main calorific resource.*

PAGE 59 *One horsepower, County Cork*

ABOVE *A natural dry dock, Dingle, County Kerry*

OPPOSITE *Dingle pier. Most of County Kerry's lobster
catch is exported to grace European menus.*

A TALE FOR EVERY DAY OF THE YEAR: VERBAL ART

BY CAOIMHÍN Ó DANACHAIR

W e Irish are talkers, and we know it. This is no mere admission, no quibble or special pleading. It is a boast, and a proud one, of a long tradition of readiness with words that has come to us down the ages. This, undoubtedly, is one of the reasons why Irish writers have made their mark so deeply in world literature, in their native language for more than twelve hundred years and in English for over two hundred, from Sheridan and Goldsmith down to the writers of today. It, unquestionably, is the reason for the large contribution to world drama by Irish playwrights, and for the fact that of all the arts, that which is most widely and most assiduously cultivated in Ireland is dramatics.

But here we are concerned with spoken words—and with our faculty for using them. For most Irish people speech is not just a bare means of communication. It is a social grace to be practiced and polished, and to be used, as a fencer uses his weapon. And the more dexterously the better—rather rapier than broadsword, rather foil than saber. To listen to the conversation of any group of people above the level of the television tongue-tied or the dissipation-drunk, in any corner of Ireland, is to witness a contest, no less fervent because it is friendly. No tactic is banned. There is, of course, a deep respect for conventional grammar, semantics, and usage, but a verbal fencer will not hesitate to split an infinitive or end a phrase with a preposition if it enhances sound or meaning. At times the outflow approaches the surreal. New phrases are developed. "A tongue that would clip a hedge" and "he'd mind mice at crossroads" are well worn by now, but new ones replace them every day. A nice sense of word meanings invents a new word where already known words do not fit the meaning precisely—this is a particular feature of Dublin speech and reminds us that Joyce's *Finnegans Wake* has a tradition behind it. These new words come and go like snowflakes in the lamplight, seldom remembered and hardly ever recorded. "Metrollops" expresses the love-hate relationship of the Dubliner to his native town—shades of *Strumpet City!* "Fusstrated" expresses his mood when he runs for a bus and misses it. The free stride of a stalwart walker is "conspacious." "Illegiterate" casts doubt on ancestry as well as on literary attainment. "Phenamadan" (a bilingual example) indicates an unusual degree of mental ineptitude. And so on. He is never at a loss for words who can coin them to suit his need. Other parts of Ireland have their own nuances of eloquence, from the sparse irony of the Northeast to the flamboyant embroidery of the Southwest.

Although the folk tradition of Ireland has, down through the centuries, showed itself in many ways—in forms of building, in skills and crafts, in social convention, in festival observance, in popular healing, in plenitude of belief and custom—its finest expression was in oral narrative, in storytelling. There is, as we may expect, a wealth of short sayings, proverbs, and epigrams, and no reluctance to change a proverb to one's need or whim: "a bird in hand needs no bush" or "a stitch in time and gone tomorrow." Verse making is a popular pursuit; poems and songs are thrown out by hundreds, and most of these are ephemeral, made only for the joy of the making, and very soon forgotten. A few find their way into writing, a very few into the permanency of print. But the prose tale was the most prized. Of course the local poet was honored, and of course almost anybody could tell a passable story, but the expert storyteller was valued above all other exponents of the verbal art.

In the Ireland of two thousand years ago, and for as long as the old Gaelic order survived, the art of the storyteller ranked equally with that of the poet and both were often combined in the same person; these arts entitled their exponents to property and privilege, land and livestock, a seat at the table with king and nobleman, and a voice in their counsels. Their proficiency came from a long course of study, up to twelve years; they were the Doctors of Literature of their time. Of course, much of their effort had to be expended on the praise and flattery of their patrons; they were experts in genealogy and could recite at length all the exploits and glories of the noble families while keeping discreet silence about their faults and failures. Their main activity, however, was the entertainment of the company at feasts and assemblies with exciting stories. The master storyteller should be ready to recite any kind of story that might be requested by lord or lady. His repertoire, we are told, should include "voyages, battles, cattle spoils, forays, courtships, elopements, pursuits, slaughters, sieges, exiles, banishments, tragedies, magic, wonders, and visions," the whole gamut of the novelists' themes.

The coming of Christian learning did little to alter this. It may have given some of the themes a more moral slant, but the churchmen fostered the ancient literary arts. Indeed, many churchmen practiced them, and the early literature is full of poems and tales ascribed to notable holy men and women. Did not Saint Patrick himself order his clerics to write down the tales of old soldiers "lest they be forgotten"? Poet and storyteller had safe-conduct and hospitality all over the country, even in time of war. Of course, it was well known that they had the opportunity, welcome among rival communities, to satirize and mock the ungenerous and the boorish in song and tale. And wasn't it always said that such a satire could raise blisters on a man's face and visibly brand him as mean and mannerless? Down even to our own day, some shreds of the uncanny cling to poet and storyteller.

The invading Vikings and Normans were caught up in the literary mesh. After all, they had their own codes of warrior courtesy, and their own skalds and troubadours. Thus, when a certain Ruaman MacColmain penetrated into Norse Dublin to entertain the Vikings with song and tale, he could demand for reward "a silver penny from every mean Norseman and two silver pennies from every generous Norseman." The Normans were overcome even more easily. From powerful earl to simple soldier, they had come to acquire estates and farms, and, incidentally, Irish wives. A couple of generations later it strained the talent of the most skilled genealogist to distinguish ethnically between the sons and daughters of a Norman man and an Irish woman and those of an Irish man and a Norman woman. The cultures mingled too. The newcomers largely adopted Irish ways and the Irish language and added to them Norman elements. Themes and modes from Continental Europe came to enrich Irish culture, while some of the Irish wealth of poem and tale passed into the general treasury of European literature.

Throughout all of this cultural commerce, the storyteller held his own, and his art flourished. This art comprised not only the tale themes but also the eloquence, the oratory, the power of dramatic delivery needed to enthrall the listeners. Nothing short of mastery of voice and gesture would suffice. Pity the tongue-tied, the hesitant, the stumbling, or the clumsy! Such presumption was hushed to silence and put to shame. The novice who showed promise was given a hearing and a critical judgment, but only the polished expert was given full approval.

Luckily for us, many of the tales were written down and form the bulk of the fictional part of our old literature. Some of the written tales appear to be original literary compositions, but many are synopses or mnemonic versions of tales intended for recital to a listening audience; these were expanded and embellished in the telling. Here we may note that the entertainment was not confined to any particular caste or class. Master and servant, rich and poor, literate and illiterate, all could listen and enjoy.

In the wars of the seventeenth century the nobility of Ireland, whether "old Irish" or "old English," were largely dispossessed and driven from their estates: Bourkes, Barrys, and Fitzgeralds as well as O'Neills, O'Connors, and O'Sullivans, and in all too many cases their places were taken by uneducated boors kicked up from the ranks of the armies of Cromwell and William of Orange. Thus died the noble patronage of art and literature that hitherto had been one of the saving graces of Irish society. Henceforth, the poet and the storyteller would practice their arts among the ordinary people; the gates of most of the "big houses" closed against them. This brought many a biting satire upon the usurpers, but with little effect; the oppressed common folk might hear them with bitter delight, but those at whom they were aimed would not appreciate the sentiment even if they understood the language. The poor became the patrons, and the Irish poets and storytellers became part of the poor, their arts sinking into the obscurity of the ordinary people's tradition, until they were rediscovered by scholars and literary men in the late nineteenth century.

In the eighteenth and nineteenth centuries another basic change became evident in Ireland. The Irish language was gradually laid aside, and its place was taken by English as the spoken tongue of the general public. Only in some small districts did Irish survive as vernacular language into the twentieth century. The nineteenth century was the time of mutation; at its start, most people in Ireland spoke Irish fluently and English hesitantly, and at its end most people spoke English fluently and Irish hardly at all. But in the mid-nineteenth century, there were people, and not a few of them, who spoke neither language well, which exposed them to much ill-informed and ill-bred "humor" in music hall and gutter press, a form of buffoonery still current in the "ethnic joke." But by the later nineteenth century the average person in Ireland had again become verbally articulate, and the art of speaking well reasserted itself as a social grace, with obvious effect upon, among others, Irish dramatists and poets.

By this time the craft of the storyteller was in decline, and the full vigor and beauty of oral narrative never passed over into English. This poses a difficulty for many who would wish to enjoy the art of the storyteller but find their way closed by a barrier of language, for the art of the storyteller still survives, although its vigor is passing away. But in the late 1800s and early 1900s there were old men and women in remote fishing villages and on lonely farms, who, like Oisin and his old warriors meeting Saint Patrick, had lived after their time, and we can understand the wonder and joy of the latter-day Patricks, people like Douglas Hyde, Lady Gregory, and John Millington Synge, on meeting and hearing these latest practitioners of narrative skills that were already old when Newgrange was raised. Imagine the rapt attention, the grasping after notebook and pencil, the effort to dash the words down on paper as they left the speaker's lips—the realization that the written word was only a very poor substitute for the oral recitation. All the warmth of character; all the nuance of voice, gesture, and rhetoric; all the personality of the storyteller —all this was lost.

Since the last decade of the nineteenth century continuous and increasing efforts, at first with notebook and pencil, more recently with various forms of mechanical dictation aids and sound-recording apparatus, have resulted in the compilation of a very great body of popular narrative, both in Irish and in English. This includes material from the repertoire of nearly every great storyteller who lived in this century. Most of this material is in written form, and has thus lost its auditory characteristics, which are, however, still preserved in the more recent sound recordings.

Many storytellers had astonishingly large repertoires. The boast of "a long tale for every day of the year," for all its echo of the *Thousand and One Nights,* was no exaggeration. Over three hundred tales have been recorded from some individuals; a stock of up to a hundred tales was commonplace, each taking from a few minutes to over an hour in the telling.

As for the subject matter of the tales, all the elements of high romance were there. Heroes set forth to seek their fortune, slaying monsters, overcoming giants, setting at naught the spells of witch and wizard. Virtue, though sorely beset, always triumphs in the end. Tyrants are humbled, oppression defeated, pride and presumptuousness chastised. There are fantastic journeys, dangers by sea and land, impossible tasks and perilous quests, but always the hero or the heroine wins through. The weak little man, by his wiles, defeats powerful and cruel enemies. The widow's son gains fame and fortune and the hand of the king's daughter. The poor forsaken maiden wins her handsome prince. Love and adventure, mystery and wonder, are all there, and always right prevails, always the wicked are punished, and the good live happily ever after.

Many of the tales are international, that is to say, they are told in many countries and languages. Some have spread into every country and every language from Ireland to Iceland to India. Where individual tales originated and how they spread is a matter for investigation by scholars, and the material gathered in Ireland is contributing to this.

In 1963, two eminent scholars, Séan Ó Súilleabháin and Reidar Christiansen, published a list of the international tales told in Ireland, *The Types of the Irish Folktale,* which gives the location of each written record of a tale. The sheer abundance of these is astonishing; the book lists nearly forty-three thousand tellings of over nine hundred international tales known in Ireland.

Of these international tales, the most popular type among Irish storytellers is the wonder tale, such as "The World Underground," "The Bird of the Golden Land," or "Cinderella," and most storytellers reveled in the wonders and the terrors. Another favorite class of tales is the romantic tale, in which there is plenty of both romance and adventure but no magical element. Tales like "The Pound of Flesh" and "The Taming of the Shrew" belong to this class. Both these themes were used by Shakespeare, but the stories were widely known centuries before his time and were told around firesides where his name was never heard.

Animal tales that told, for instance, how the wren became King of the Birds, or how the clever fox stole the peddler's fish, were also popular in Ireland, as were humorous anecdotes like that of Séan na Scuab, the simpleton seller of brooms who, by chance, became mayor of Limerick and surprised even himself with the wisdom of his pronouncements.

As popular and widespread as these international tales were in Ireland, they were still outnumbered and outclassed by the great body of stories native to Ireland. Foremost of these, and among the best traditional tales of the whole world, are the Fenian tales, or hero tales, which recount the deeds and adventures of Fionn MacCumhail (Finn MacCoul) and his warrior band and of other ancient heroes. Some of these, such as "The Pursuit of Diarmuid and Gráinne" and "Deirdre of the Sorrows," have passed into modern literature, while others, like "Conal Gulban" and "The Palace of the Quicken Trees," are hardly known outside the circle of the folktale enthusiasts. There are also great numbers of Irish wonder and romantic tales. There are tales of saints and hermits, of rogues and simpletons, of hapless lovers, henpecked husbands and patient wives, of animals, ghosts, and fairies, of sea monsters, sunken cities, and hidden treasure.

Local tales abound, and they are always worth inquiry. There is scarcely a hill, a rock, or river pool, a ruined castle or abbey, which doesn't have its own story. Why this road bends to avoid an ancient earthwork, why that house is haunted, why the tree stands bare but its shadow on the moonlit road shows a body swinging by a rope—all these are part of the oral currency of the countryside.

We must remember that all these tales were intended for the entertainment of adult audiences, although children, too, listened to them with pleasure. Before the penetration of modern media of entertainment into the countryside, the folktale took the place now filled by the glossy magazine, the novel, the radio, and the television, not forgetting, of course, the theater and the cinema. With the coming into the countryside of all of these, the storytellers have lost most of their audience to the newer forms of entertainment. There still are storytellers, but now they must be sought out and coaxed to tell their tales, where formerly they held court night after night—especially in the long winter nights.

More than anyone else, the storytellers of the past must take the credit for the perfecting of the verbal art. They were required to be good at stringing words. The audience was severely critical, and though shortcomings of an apprentice to the art might be tolerated, none but the truly expert could gain honor. The poor storyteller soon lost his audience and, moreover, earned scorn and contempt as one who had set himself above his station in an art beyond his talents.

Because of recent research, we know more now than ever before about the storyteller's art, while at the same time the storytellers themselves are disappearing from the scene. Perhaps, however, this is only a temporary eclipse. The 1960s and 1970s saw an astonishing and quite unexpected revival of Irish folk music. The verbal art is far from dead and an audience jaded by the vapidity of television entertainment may well turn again to the most ancient of verbal skills, that of the storyteller, and give new life to a form of art that reaches back in time beyond any record of memory.

BETWEEN IRISH AND BRITISH FIDELITIES: POETRY

BY SEAMUS DEANE

The first volume in the modern tradition of Irish poetry in the English language was a series of translations from the Irish. The book was *Reliques of Irish Poetry*, the translator was Charlotte Brooke, and the year of publication was 1789, the year of the French Revolution. The original Irish was printed alongside the translations. The purpose of the volume was to introduce the British audience to the rich Gaelic literary culture and to invigorate English poetry with the energies of this fresh resource. Charlotte Brooke imagined the British and Irish muses as "sweet ambassadresses of cordial union between two countries that seem formed by nature to be joined by every bond of interest and unity." The historical importance of this work is enhanced in retrospect when we note the political implications of its avowed aim and of its date; the relationship between poetry and the politics of the Irish–British situation was to be sustained for the next two centuries. In addition, the emphasis on the connection between the revival of the Irish language and the revival of literature in English was to be repeated at the end of the nineteenth century, as the Irish Renaissance got under way. The coexistence of the two languages and the tension between them, modulated in a great variety of translations all through the nineteenth and into the twentieth century, remained a salient feature of the Irish sensibility and of Irish writing up to the present. After Charlotte Brooke, Anglo–Irish poetry emerged as a body of work uneasily poised between two languages and cultures, drawing much of its strength from Gaelic culture, which was almost completely destroyed by the mid-century famine, and directing much of its attention to a British audience invincibly ignorant of the drastic conditions that British policy had generated in Ireland. In a sense, before Yeats and Lady Gregory appeared on the scene, most Irish poetry in English was translation, the aim of which was to recover within the forms natural to English something of the heritage and power native to the Irish language. So Thomas Moore's *Irish Melodies*, published in ten separate numbers between 1807 and 1834, was an attempt to adapt Irish music to the English language in such a way that the British audience would be won over to a more sympathetic appreciation of Ireland's plight. Moore was certainly servile and sentimental by turns. But his *Melodies* became famous all over the world and were astonishingly popular in nineteenth-century Ireland. For he recognized what he called the connection between "politics and music," expressed in Ireland in the political and sentimental ballads from which the tradition of poetry has sometimes recruited its strength or against which it has tried to define itself. After Moore, the most popular book of verse in nineteenth-century Ireland was the collection of ballads that had first been published in Thomas Davis's newspaper *The Nation*, founded in 1842. This collection, which first appeared in 1843 under the title *The Spirit of the Nation*, reached its fiftieth edition in 1870. It was much more militant in tone than Moore's *Melodies*, which had made the beauty of the Irish landscape and its many ruins a matter of nostalgic longing and regret for what had irretrievably passed away. The vacillation between this attitude and the more rebellious and angry militarism of *The Spirit of the Nation* was itself a symptom of the fluctuations in Irish political opinion in that period. When they were being sentimental and charmingly volatile, the Irish were "Celtic"; when they were rebellious and militant, they were Fenians.

Apart from Moore and Davis, the other important poets were Sir Samuel Ferguson, an Ulster Protestant Unionist, a translator of genius, and a sponsor of the idea that, by recovering their lost Gaelic culture through the English language, the Irish could learn "to *live back*, in the land they live *in*"; and James Clarence Mangan, best remembered as the author of *Dark Rosaleen*, the epitome of the Irish romantic poet. Addicted to drugs, oppressed by poverty, lost in obscurity, given to what he called "translations" from a variety of languages, including Irish, none of which he knew in the original, Mangan has become the prototype of the Irish artist victimized by political and social circumstances, dedicated to solitude and alien to the conventional world in which he lived. His death from cholera at the height of the Great Famine finally certified his tragic appeal for later Irish writers. Both Joyce and Yeats were fascinated by him and saw him as an omen for their own careers.

One generation after the famine had decimated the Irish population and in the decade in which Parnell's downfall had disheartened the Irish in their drive for Home Rule, the astonishing Irish Revival, as it is now called, took place. A small island, with a population of something like five million people, devastated by poverty, violence, and all the evil effects of colonial rule, suddenly produced a literature of world importance in the English language, even as it was attempting to recover from the traumatic loss of its own. It is, perhaps, not surprising that the great Irish writers of the generation that flourished between 1880 and 1930 should be remembered, above all, for their linguistic virtuosity. They had, as a consequence of their immediate history, a sensitivity to language and a determination to master it that arose directly from their sense of their peculiar estrangement from it. For they wrote in English and were not English; they were Irish and did not write in Irish. Translation had done what it could to mediate this crisis. After 1880, translation, while still practiced, gave up its primacy to an almost vengeful virtuosity. Even a roll call of the names indicates this sudden turn—Shaw, Wilde, George Moore, Joyce, Yeats, Synge, O'Casey, Beckett. All of them are, in their different ways, experimental, even avant-garde, writers. Ireland experienced the phenomenon of producing a highly sophisticated, modernist literature within a culture that was economically backward and provincially isolated. With this writing there also came, in the same generations, a political revolution, starting with the Land League and coming to term with the rise of Sinn Féin and the war of the Irish Republican Army against the British from 1919 until 1921. The new Irish State came into being. The Celtic Twilight of the young Yeats had given way to the dawn of a new dispensation.

Neither Yeats nor many of the other writers of the 1930s especially liked this new dispensation, even though they had contributed to its formation. After the thirties, Irish writers in the new state began their long battle with the stifling censorship and pieties of the Catholic middle-class society, which had triumphantly emerged from the miseries of the last century. Austin Clarke and Patrick Kavanagh reacted angrily to the new situation. The poetry of both these men is, perhaps, weakened by the satiric intent that governs a great deal of it. But Clarke, after a long period in which he lived under the shadow of Yeats, finally broke free and found, not only his own voice, but his own theme—the strength of religious belief and prescriptions and instinctual longing, the hunger for a culture that would successfully reconcile the two. This was a theme that was entirely representative of a central dilemma of the new state. Clarke's exploration of it in verse that had absorbed many of the intricate techniques of Gaelic poetry is still a monumental achievement. Clarke's final dismissal of the Yeatsian influence did not take place until 1961. Kavanagh, on the other hand, had by then waged a long war against the fake idealization of Irish life—especially that of the peasant—which seemed to him to be a central part of the great "lie" of the Irish Revival. Kavanagh, in saying this, was doing something more than undergoing the routine reaction of one generation against its predecessor. He was also announcing the end of the Anglo–Irish literature as such and the appearance of an indigenous literature in the English language, which would be preoccupied with the plain realities of Irish life rather than with metaphysical maunderings about the essential features of "Irishness." Only for those who were troubled by it, like the Anglo–Irish, could that problem of "identity," that wavering between the Irish and English fidelities, be a central preoccupation. Yet Kavanagh's rather brutal repudiation was in many ways premature, even if crucial for later Irish poetry. As a poet, his own most remarkable achievement was to announce the triumph of the local and the ordinary element in human experience over the esoteric and extraordinary, which Yeats had exploited with incomparable skill and power. For Kavanagh, to know with intimacy your own parish was to come into contact with the universal. In a dozen or so poems, most of them belonging to the early 1960s, Kavanagh achieves the celebratory vision that had been implicit in much of his early work and that now stands as a more enduring alternative to the shabby Ireland he had depicted in his satiric and journalistic writings.

The bitter sense of provincial shutdown experienced by the writers of the 1940s and 1950s encouraged many of them to search for a more cosmopolitan, less strictly localized, frame of reference. Prominent among those who found a release through this discovery of the transnational character of late modernist literature were Samuel Beckett, Denis Devlin, Brian Coffey, and Thomas Kinsella. As a poet, Kinsella is the outstanding member of this group. His work has been influenced by the example and achievement of Ezra Pound. Dense and difficult, it is a series of sustained meditations on history and the nature of creativity. Shadowed by a depressed sense of the incoherence of both specifically Irish and general human experience, it is invigorated by the belief in the structuring, ordering capacity of art. Only Yeats has achieved a comparable intensity in his preoccupation with these matters. Kinsella's contemporary, John Montague, also sought escape from the provincialism of the Irish scene by residences abroad in the United States and France, searching for relief from the oppressions of the depressed Ireland of the 1950s in the literary culture of these two leading countries in the international modernist movement.

Then came the 1960s. Everything suddenly changed in Ireland. For those living it, the change was at first hardly perceptible. Although I can now see the links that tie the present generation of writers to the past I have described above, the recognition was a long time in coming. This was inevitable. It took me an unconscionably long time to realize that I lived in a ghetto. I began to come to political consciousness at about the same time I became aware of literature. The two have never been separate for me since. In the normal way of things, a literary tradition, or the idea of it, dawned very slowly. I was at school in Derry with Seamus Heaney. Later we were undergraduates together at university in Belfast. For both of us, poetry was something written by other people—Vergil, Ronsard, Wordsworth. We liked it but felt it remote. The Irish achievement in literature was at first unknown to us. Poems were little more than half-embarrassed exchanges of verse on exercise books. Yet the pressure of events and the pressure of reading both told in the end and, just as we were about to leave the university, we both, in different ways, recognized that writing had become a commitment for us. At the same time, Northern Ireland began to fall apart. The isolation of young writers then was hard to believe. Derek

Mahon tells of entering a poetry competition in the confident belief that he would win because he was sure no one else in Ireland was writing poetry. He was astounded to learn that someone called John Montague took the prize. Even as the northern renaissance began—with Heaney, Mahon, Longley, Simmons, and others, I left Ireland for Cambridge and temporarily forsook poetry for the pleasures of scholarly research. Poetry, however, would not go away. I continued to scribble and began to become aware of the Irish writers whom I was now reading in England with a sense of discovery. But I was still ignorant of Kinsella, Kavanagh, Montague, Devlin, and all the others. Only when Seamus Heaney arrived on my doorstep in Cambridge one evening with his first book, *Death of a Naturalist*, and a literary prize under his arm, did I begin to realize that poetry was something we had a share in, no longer a remote wonder achieved by others. A two-year sojourn in the United States put an end to my implacable isolation from the contemporary scene. At the University of California in Berkeley, I met many of the American poets of the 1960s and, oddly, began at last to read the Irish poets of the 1950s and of my own generation. The excitements of that decade are now long past, but they left a deep imprint. Literature never again had for me that enchanted distance from the real that had made it so attractive before. Now I realized how deeply and harshly it demanded of writers the necessity to live in the present without being imprisoned by it.

When I returned to Ireland from a Berkeley under curfew and full of tear gas, I spent my first weekend in Derry. It was October 1968. The occasion was the first civil rights march. Once again, people were running from the police, batons were swinging, and TV cameras were purring. I had arrived at a crucial time. Four years later, Derry had Bloody Sunday. In between, the bloodletting in the North had begun in earnest. The only response I could make was through poetry. Then for the first time I began to feel a member of a generation afflicted by a historical crisis and, again for the first time, I began to have a sense of what Irish writing had, for centuries, been grappling to overcome. When history becomes coincident with biography, poetry emerges. That has happened now in the North for that generation which reached maturity before 1970. All of us are confronted by the fact that the Northern troubles, so called, supplied our desire to write with a powerful impulse, just as it also gave our writing a visibility that it might otherwise not have had. From Charlotte Brooke through to Yeats, poetry of the island had been rooted in a culture's apparently unending crises. Yet, even in recognizing our kinship with the past in this respect, we also recognized that it brought with it other responsibilities. Literature, especially poetry, had so often been offered as a means of healing divisions, or as a means of overcoming them by bringing them into the deep magnetic fields of the imagination's free space. For me, one of the questions that still remain unanswered concerns the legitimacy of poetry as an activity in itself. Can it be something other than a parasitic growth on the general crisis? Can it have a function within this squalor and despair that is so prevalent in the North? It is a strange thing to recognize that the solitude out of which poetry grows is transformed, by the act of writing and of publishing, into a sense of communion with an audience which is sensitive to that solitude because it has known it so long. The grief of the best poems that have emerged in the North—in Derek Mahon's *A Disused Shed in County Wicklow*, in John Montague's *The Rough Field*, in Seamus Heaney's *North* and *Field Work*, most especially in the Glanmore sonnet sequence in that last volume—is the North's truest note. My admiration for and love of poetry are rooted in the realization that nowhere else will that grief ever find comparable articulation. It is a grief that endures but does not desolate because it is a grief that men have mastered. In that, poetry achieves its freedom and in that, modern Irish poetry aligns itself with the long and tragic condition which the Gaelic poets of the seventeenth and eighteenth centuries and Charlotte Brooke, in the year of the French Revolution, gave us as an inescapable possession, a central sighting of our inheritance.

FROM THE ENCHANTED POOL: PROSE

BY BENEDICT KIELY

Irish prose fiction in our century begins, like the river Shannon itself, in an enchanted pool. "Every lake is a mystery, except the lakes that are merely expansions, overflowing of a great river, like the Shannon lakes, and whosoever is born in a lake district and has lived on lake shores never loses sight of lakes, however far he may wander from them. . . ."

That was, of course, George Moore, in that exquisite historical novel, *Ulick and Soracha*. A few pages farther on he writes of a mild and gracious lake amid low shores vanishing into great distances, the lake curving around the island fortresses and forests.

Moore welded that novel into his one joyous book, *A Storyteller's Holiday*, with an acknowledgment to Balzac for the aptness of the adjective and the suggestion that every writer should write at least one joyous book.

In *Ulick and Soracha* Moore mingled past and present, the living, moving lake and the gray, hoary castle on the island. And in the character of Ulick de Burgo, wandering to Europe in search of song, Moore saw himself as the young man in Paris in search of art. It was there that he expressed, in his highest prose, his most perfect use of what he pedantically called the melodic line, his undying nostalgia for Lough Carra. Moore's best Irish novel he called unashamedly *The Lake* and insisted that every man had a lake in his heart—against, it would seem to me, the natural claims on other men of the river, the mountain, or rapture on the lonely shore.

Frank O'Connor, who had every right to speak on the matter, said that the modern Irish short story began in George Moore's collection, *The Untilled Field*. It is a statement that calls for some slight qualification, as does the statement in the very title of the Moore collection, implying that he was breaking his way through the brambles, rooting out weeds and thistles, overturning dead earth, planting a new, unique crop. This was an arrogant claim, but not quite unjustified and no more arrogant than the claim of the young James Joyce, which in this case we may equate with the claim of Stephen Dedalus:

"So be it. Welcome, O life! I go to encounter for the millionth time the reality of my experience and to forge in the smithy of my soul the uncreated conscience of my race. . . ." Yet we may allow much for the arrogance of the young, or of the artist thinking to stand apart paring his nails, or simply of the writer of fiction, with something of what Graham Greene calls the ice in the blood, speaking for his people whether they wish him to or not.

Young Stephen had meditated on the cloistral, silver-veined prose of John Henry Newman. And Joyce perhaps took the inspiration of that prose with him from the place in the center of Dublin where Newman had taught to other cities—Paris, Trieste, Zurich —and in a prose as exact as geometry he re-created the city as few writers of prose or poetry had ever done. (Ironically, perhaps, or fittingly, the bust of Newman and the bust of Joyce are today to be seen within a short distance of each other in Dublin.)

Moore too had walked in that city, casting on it the cold eye of a man called Moore, a proper gent, who lived on his property's ten percent and wrote about it sadly enough in his novel *A Drama in Muslin*, more mellowly perhaps, in *Hail and Farewell*. A passage in *Muslin* and a passage in the long story "The Dead," in which the Joycean city is abandoned for the dream of a westward journey, link the two writers in a curious way.

In *Muslin* the young woman Alice Barton stands at the window of a big house of the gentry in the West and looks out at the snow desolately falling, an image of her own spiritual desolation: "But through her virgin eyes the plain of virginal snow, flecked with the cold blue shadows of the trees, sank into her soul, bleaching it of every hope of joy; and, gathering suggestions from her surroundings, she saw a white path extending before her—a sterile way that she would have to tread—a desolate way, with no songs in its sullen air, but only sad sighs, and only stainless tears, falling, falling, ever falling—falling silently. Grey was the gloom that floated, and overworn were the spectres that passed therein; and the girl buried her face in her hands, as if to shut out the vision of the journey she would have to go."

At the splendid ending of Joyce's story "The Dead," Gabriel Conroy looks, as we all know, through the window of a hotel bedroom in Dublin and sleepily watches the snowflakes, silver and dark, falling obliquely against the lamplight, and thinks of a faraway Connacht graveyard and of the hapless boy his wife had loved in her girlhood and mourned forever after.

Was the younger and later writer subtly, even humorously, acknowledging a debt that he was never willing to admit in straight statement? Or, more likely, was he wishing to show that anything Moore could do, he could do better?

After George Moore came God's plenty both in the novel and the short story, which is not to say that he was responsible for that plenitude, but he, like the Word, was there in the beginning.

In 1950 I pasted together a lot of previously written articles and previously spoken radio talks and had the audacity to call the result a book, *Modern Irish Fiction*. I found that, patchy and incomplete as the thing was, I had still touched on about fifty Irish writers, none of them unworthy of attention, who had been working in the novel and the short story in the previous thirty years.

In 1950, and in a pretty obvious effort to mask my own deficiency, yet with some justification, I wrote: "The writing of this book has been to a large extent a journey across uncharted country, and there will be many opinions as to how the first road across such country should be made and the direction it should follow."

Thirty-odd years later the justification is more true than ever. Very little work of assessment has been done. Examples and efforts are too few to mention. One may pitifully ape that Joycean angel (acknowledgment to Wyndham Lewis) and fly over the land from Rathlin to Spike Island, from Inishmore to St. Stephen's Green, considering the West through the eyes of Seamus O'Kelly, Liam O'Flaherty; the Midlands through the eyes of Brinsley MacNamara, Mary Lavin, John Broderick; coasting around the upper half of the island with the aid of Patrick MacGill, Peadar O'Donnell, Brian Friel, Pat Boyle, Michael McLaverty, Bernard McLaverty, Maurice Leitch, Sam Hanna Bell, Joe Tomelty, Brian Moore, Forrest Reid. There are special visions in Francis Stuart, Elizabeth Bowen, John Banville, Aidan Higgins, Jack B. Yeats, and Samuel Beckett. And with the inspiration of Isaac Babel and Ivan Turgenev and under the tuition of Daniel Corkery, Cork declared its own republic in O'Connor and O'Faolain, and the gates of Dublin are well opened by Flann O'Brien. James Stephens and O'Casey in his *Autobiographies* and James Plunkett and Anthony Cronin living the life of Riley will, for the moment, be guides good enough.

My own approach to prose-fiction was not by way of a lake, and no offense to Mr. Moore. But I hold with Edmund Blunden that:

> Some love the mountains, some the sea,
> But a river-god is the god for me.

In a public park on the Camowen River before it reaches the town of Omagh, in County Tyrone, a park called the Lover's Retreat but known by a grosser name to the liberal soldiers in the barracks, I met, one evening in 1936, a young fusilier. We became friendly over the next few months, then he disappeared for a while, and I next met him being escorted from the railway station by two Royal Ulster constables. In the relaxed atmosphere of those days it was possible to stop and ask them what it was all about. It appeared that my pal had deserted from the army and, while heading for the border at Strabane, made love to some bits of property that did not belong to him, such as a bicycle, a suit of clothes, and so on. He was very cheerful about it all and was on the best terms with his captors.

I never saw him again, but I did not forget him and, even if I have long forgotten his name, I can still see him laughing on the way to jail. About the time of Christmas of 1939 I started to write a story about him under the title "King's Shilling." I suppose I could say very grandly that my runaway soldier was the symbol of the pilgrim soul and that I was trying to express something very deep about the plight of man on earth. But then I wasn't trying to make him seem to be anything of the sort. I was merely trying to write down the joy I felt in the valley of the Stule River, to which the Camowen contributes, when the grass meadows were going down in June or July. So I set my soldier running away along that valley.

There naturally had to be people in the story or it wouldn't be a story at all, and I really did like the original of the soldier. The effort of trying to get him down on paper was well worthwhile. The other people came to mind as easily as grass grew. They also had grown in the valley. It never occurred to me that the people were different from myself. Why should it have? But grass and the river and Bessy Bell Mountain above it were different: People passed, they remained.

In these unpropitious times the complications of the life of that river valley and elsewhere in Ulster have sadly manifested themselves. Writers in the coming times will tell of that manifestation. But even the greediest novelist with the most ice in his blood might prefer it otherwise.

PAGE 81   *O'Brien's Tower, Cliffs of Moher, County Clare*
PAGES 82 AND 83   *Slea Head, Dingle Peninsula, County Kerry*
ABOVE   *Where the mountains of Mourne sweep down to the sea, County Down*
OPPOSITE   *Under bare Ben Bulben's head is the grave of the poet W. B. Yeats, County Sligo*
PAGES 86 AND 87   *The Wicklow hills*

ABOVE LEFT *Poppies, County Carlow*

ABOVE RIGHT *Caisearbhán, the Irish for dandelion, can also mean
"a sour person." The leaves are sometimes used in salads.*

OPPOSITE *In the Sperrin Mountains, County Tyrone*

Bangor, County Down: a resort and residential suburb

A new housing development, Portballintrae, County Antrim

ABOVE *Trim, County Meath. The Anglo-Norman castle,*
the largest in the country, was founded by Hugh de Lacy in 1173.

BELOW *Eight hundred years later: a suburban scene, Trim, County Meath*

OPPOSITE, ABOVE *Londonderry from across the river Foyle*

OPPOSITE, BELOW *Eighteenth-century decorum: Hillsborough, County Down*

ABOVE *Streetscape near Queen's University, Belfast*

OPPOSITE, ABOVE *Sandymount, a residential suburb on Dublin's south shore*

OPPOSITE, BELOW *Suburban setting, Belfast*

ABOVE *Londonderry. The walls were built between 1617 and 1619.*

LEFT *Expectant twins, Newtownstewart, County Tyrone*

OPPOSITE *Soles and heels, Thomastown, County Kilkenny*

Rural architecture, County Limerick

AT THE EDGE OF THE OLD WORLD

BY PETER SOMERVILLE-LARGE

In the twelfth century the Welsh monk Giráldus Cambrensis visited Ireland and found it "uneven, mountainous, soft, woody, exposed to winds and so boggy that you might see the water stagnating on the mountains." Giraldus was the first traveler to convey something of the mosaic quality of the Irish landscape. Today, in a world shrunk by modern communication, Ireland is a tiny place, and yet it gives an impression of immensity by the diversity of its thirty-two counties. Go down any boreen, take any fugitive road, and you will be surprised. You may find a stretch of land like the patch in East Galway that still looks as Thomas Carlyle saw it over a century ago: "Fifteen miles of the stoniest barest barrenness I have ever seen." By contrast it will not take you long to come upon the rich pastures of the Golden Vale or the prosperous plains of Kildare and Meath or the fertile farms of Wexford.

Mountain ranges so numerous they would take up a page of beautiful names to list —Slieve Bloom, Slievefelim, Slievenaman, Silvermines, Ballyhoura, Galty, Comeragh, Knockmealdown, Mourne, Sperrin, Glenbeigh, Blue Stack, and so on—are threaded by scores of brown and silver rivers, while the country is divided by the complexities of the river Shannon and Lough Erne. Killarney on a spring morning is remembered by the reflection of the lakes and the bright green flush of new leaves. Lough Gur with its ancient crannogs offers the legend of the damned earl and his horse with silver shoes. The basalt hexagons of the Giant's Causeway in County Antrim, the result of ancient volcanic fumings and coolings, provided nineteenth-century thinkers with evidence that nature was not only divine, but could do as well as art. The glens of Antrim, linked by the roller coaster Coast Road, offer a serenity belied by recent history. The gentians and the starry flowers of the Burren in County Clare, growing beside the limestone, reflect in miniature the lushness and the barrenness of Ireland's landscapes. Much more variety is crowded into an area the size of Pennsylvania.

The island's position at the edge of the Old World adds to the dramatic quality of its scenery. We cannot be unaware of how Europe comes to an end among the ragged peninsulas of West Cork, beside the Fastnet Rock, which emigrants, sailing by on their way to America, remembered as the Tear Drop of Ireland. The sea contributed to the preservation of Christianity during the Dark Ages, when from islands and hilltops, and from the Skellig Rocks, "the most westerly of Christ's fortresses," saints and hermits linked the mysteries of the trackless ocean with their religion. After years of contemplating storms and the sparkle of the sun on the ocean, Saint Brendan came down from his aerie on Mount Brandon and embarked toward the West. Like the saints, we can look upon views that cleanse earthly desires, lying on a bank of heather near the shore, perhaps listening to a lark singing to the accompaniment of waves.

Our fourth dimension is the weather, governed by the North Atlantic Drift, which comes close to our western shores and keeps the climate mild. The result is an astonishing cloudland offering some of the same diversity as the land below. We are kept on a razor edge of uncertainty while fat cumulous clouds such as those Paul Henry painted are driven across the sun to make way for the rain givers. Giraldus wrote an early complaint: "There is such a plentiful supply of rain . . . such an ever-present overhanging of clouds and fog that you will scarcely see even in summer consecutive days of really fine weather." He may have visited during a bad summer, like Heinrich Böll, eight centuries later, who rejoiced in the downpour: "The rain here is absolute, magnificent, and frightening. To call this rain bad weather is as inappropriate as to call scorching sunshine fine weather."

Rain is remembered longer than the other moods of climate—the movement, color, and substance of a day's progress and the shifting green light that absorbs some of the nacreous quality of the clouds. From a train window the clouds will change as often as the scenes of passing sheep and cattle. The brightest day and sky is uncertain, so that the occasional week of summer heat, when the footprints of cattle harden to rock and the willows go brown, has a feeling of the miraculous.

In this unique, restless climate the land has had human occupation for a relatively short time—it is roughly nine thousand years since the first settlers crossed from Wales and Scotland to live precariously on the shores of Antrim and Dublin Bay, where their middens have been found. Traces of man's past cross a wide time span from the ring forts stamped on fertile hillsides to the hawthorn tree in the middle of a field left unharmed by the tractor, the Norman castle used as a cattle byre, and the furrows under the bracken, like ribs of a starving man, marking old potato beds.

The achievements of Neolithic society could not be proclaimed more dramatically than by the tumuli of Newgrange and Dowth beside the river Boyne. Elsewhere more modest signs of prehistory are prominent enough—a pillar with ogham writing, a dolmen or a stone circle aligned to the winter solstice. Christianity lightly superimposed itself upon the pagan world: a cross scratched on a pillar stone, a well—already holy because the source of water is always divine—associated with a Christian saint. Often architecture has fused with its surroundings, so that the beehive huts of the Skelligs cannot be separated from their incredible location, Gallarus Oratory from the cliffs of Dingle, the round tower from the lake at Glendalough, or Cashel from its limestone knuckle rising out of the Tipperary plain.

A field may be molded by a thousand years of farming, or it may have been hacked out of forest. As late as the sixteenth century much of Ireland was covered in forest. The oaks were felled by the invading Planter for charcoal. There are just a few places left, like Killarney and Glengarriff, where we can enter the communion with nature enjoyed by the monk in his "leafy desert."

> In a grey mantle from the top of bushes
> The cuckoo sings:
> Verily—may the Lord shield me—
> Well do I write under the greenwood.

No one could write well under a stand of Norwegian spruce. Fir trees, now all too common a feature of the countryside, planted as deliberate commercial policy in sour mountain land, are poor replacements for the oak, hazel, and holly of the medieval forest. They are the latest indication of accelerating change in the landscape.

Some small introductions, initially insignificant, have managed to transform the appearance of large sections of the countryside. Until the last quarter of the nineteenth century the fuchsia, a native of Patagonia, was unusual enough to be called to the traveler's attention. Now its hedges thrive in the moist climate of the West, becoming as much a part of the Irish scene as the donkey—another nineteenth-century import. The rhododendron has joyfully returned after its extinction during the Ice Age. Tens of thousands of years later it was brought back to Ireland as a garden exotic and found itself at home. Now it is a weed of the countryside, a showy menace threatening native trees.

Ireland has not escaped pollution. Lakes have become toxic, uncontrolled town planning has scarred the outskirts of towns and cities, while beauty spots have their quota of derelict cars and burst rubbish bags. Prosperity has meant that the cottage has given way to the bungalow, but the aesthetically minded are reluctant to accept chocolate-colored tiles, rising-sun motifs, and grisilinia hedging as substitutes for the picturesque thatch and hens of the past. Wildlife is threatened by greed or by modern farming techniques. The corncrake, the peregrine, the fox—hunted for its pelt—and even the lordly salmon may go the way of the lemming, the reindeer, and the wolf. Other species are imperiled by the extinction of their habitats. Although there are still stretches of bog where the sphagnum moss swells in the wet like yeast, wetlands may succumb to drainage and to modern turf-cutting techniques.

But on the whole we have been lucky not to be more affected by the ravages of civilization. This is partly because the country is underpopulated, the lack of numbers a bitter heritage of history. Another progression of history has brought about the recent transfer of land. The landlord's walled estate with its scattering of beeches and cawing rooks has become a rarity.

In this century possession of land has been of passionate importance. The farm has not only been a symbol of status but also a trophy of a slowly fought, hard-won political and social victory. David Thompson has noted: "What land means to a peasant people —that love of it—can be more jealous than love of a woman and more steadfast because it is embedded in the past."

In a rural society the strong sense of "our place"—as opposed to the outside world —has been another emotional tie to a particular patch of ground. "Our place" may well be among the most beautiful places in the world. Perhaps it is a farm in the wilds of Mayo or on a mountain in Donegal or in West Cork. From the parlor window of the farmhouse you can see the mountains and the sea. There is a shimmer of water and a view of distant islands with perhaps the gray stump of a castle that was abandoned by the farmer's ancestors centuries ago. Now he will have thirty or forty acres, and this is the land that matters. Every square inch is important to him and to his thirty cows.

The almost mystical belief in the right to land ownership has been challenged by those who believe that land should be looked after and that those who neglect their reed-filled fields do not necessarily retain a God-given privilege to hold on to them. The harsh facts of modern economics intrude. This is not an attitude that has made much headway, since the right to own land has been too recently won to be considered as possibly forfeit. Even if the younger farmer is easing up on the passion that bound his father to the soil, the old hunger induced by alien rule, landlord rents, and nationalism will still be strong.

But the new generation will have a more pragmatic attitude to farming. There is less emphasis on rural tradition and more talk of European Economic Community grants and the cost of fertilizer. If the farmer and his wife are in their forties, they will have been the last generation to have endured "the slavery"—the harsh routines of the past. The drudgery of taking the bucket to the well, or lighting the lamps, or of relying on a horse and cart for transport has at last ceased. The house and farmyard show the signs of progress: the television, the car, and the milking parlor. The fields have been drained and enlarged to make way for modern machinery, while hedges are ripped out. A gradual revolution is taking place as the shape of the land changes once again.

For all the changes, for so much that would be unrecognizable to Giraldus, there is much that remains constant—the bones of the land, the mountains and hills, the wandering rivers, and the sea, which never seems quite out of earshot, caressing the coastline until it is at harmony with the green center, like the painted rim of a plate.

BECOMING URBANIZED FROM THE OUTSIDE

BY PATRICK SHAFFREY

In the visual sense, the traditional view of Ireland, and not the least in American eyes, is a romantic one: a land of superb scenery—mountain, coastline, lake, and river; of country cottages and small farms; of round towers, ruined castles and abbeys. It is essentially a rural one—memories of a past society. This view was no doubt fashioned by the nineteenth-century émigrés, who were mostly from the countryside. The Irish image—with the main exception of Dublin, the principal city, seat of government, and gateway to the country—is different from that of Continental Europe. There the essential image is of great cities and ancient towns steeped in history and full of charm and character, of interesting buildings, large and small. Dublin's international fame rests principally on the architectural qualities of its eighteenth- and nineteenth-century streets and squares with their many elegant public buildings, mostly dating from the eighteenth century. Many people, and sadly many Dubliners also, now feel that the architectural aspects of Dublin's reputation have been greatly diminished in recent years, despite the valiant battles fought by conservation groups and, at times, by the general mass of citizens. This was perhaps due to a combination of facts: the intense pressure for development after many years of stagnation; a lack of appreciation of the essential character of the city and its international architectural status; and, perhaps most significantly of all, a narrow view of what might be classified as "Irish culture."

This traditional view of Ireland was also held for years, within Ireland itself, by the establishment and indeed by many ordinary citizens. The essential culture and identity of Ireland were associated with political ideas, music, and language. The importance of the visual arts and crafts was ignored, or at best underestimated. The view of architecture was perhaps even more blinkered, in addition to a general unconcern about its importance as a social art. The great mass of notable buildings—the great country houses, fine Georgian streets, and impressive public buildings, erected before the foundation of the state in 1922—were often considered as not being expressive of an Irish culture, but rather as the physical expression of a society gone and unlamented. The twin pillars, which for many years supported the notion of an ideal culture, were in concept both Gaelic and Catholic. This was difficult ground indeed in which to sow the seeds of a new vision that would first recognize the relevance of the architectural and building heritage—and its comprehensive nature.

However, in recent years there have been many encouraging changes. The essential culture and the distinctiveness of any country or society are now recognized as multifaceted, having strands, all making a contribution. This new outlook is one result of a developing society with higher standards and different approaches to education. Perhaps most significantly, we are now looking outward and learning from other countries. Travelers to Continental Europe have been impressed by the manner in which cities and towns were rebuilt after the wars and by the care and appreciation that is extended to the architectural heritage. They discover that many fine buildings and towns were also built by the foreign powers of the day, or by societies now also gone and largely unlamented, but that this does not reduce their architectural or historical significance.

Irish people are now beginning to see their towns and buildings in a new light. Old buildings, whether they are churches, market houses, or just small dwellings, are more widely appreciated. There is concern about the loss of an old building, or the effect that a new one might have on its neighbors. This is part of a worldwide trend in which a general disquiet about the standards and effects of most modern architecture stimulated an awareness of past styles.

So what is this essential architectural heritage to which I have been alluding? Ireland has an urban tradition somewhat different from that of other European countries. Geographically isolated, it was not influenced by Roman civilization nor was it situated on the great trade and religious pilgrimage routes of medieval Europe. This does not mean, however, that there are no towns of great antiquity. A number of Irish cities and towns were founded by the Vikings, and so are at least a thousand years old, perhaps older. All these earlier settlements are on the coastline, as is to be expected on an island that became "urbanized" from the outside, rather than as a process of internal development.

The Normans, who arrived toward the end of the twelfth century, built on the earlier Viking foundations. The number of specifically Norman towns, such as Carrickfergus, Trim, Athenry, and Kilkenny, is probably few. However, the Normans established religious institutions, developed markets, and generally gave the towns an administrative and commercial basis. Despite all the wars and disturbances of history, the process of building and shaping towns was a continuous one. Few, if any, traces of the old Viking foundations, or indeed Norman ones, remain today, although the atmosphere associated with medieval towns—narrow streets, mixed land use: shops, offices, and public buildings side by side—can still be experienced.

In broad general terms, however, urban development did not commence on any significant scale until the seventeenth century, with the founding, on confiscated lands, of the Ulster Plantation towns. These rather basic urban centers were also affected by the later political disturbances of the seventeenth century, and there are a few tangible remains today. Modern urban development, as we know it, began in the eighteenth century and continued practically uninterrupted until the middle of the nineteenth century. During that period, Dublin in particular saw a century of more or less continuous building. It was the second city in the kingdom of Britain and Ireland, and, architecturally, among the most graceful cities of Europe. In the provincial towns, development commenced somewhat later, and the great period, particularly in smaller towns, was at the beginning of the nineteenth century. In a time span of not more than forty years, the physical form and layout of many towns, as we know them today, was established—a tremendous achievement in building and estate development even by today's standards.

Ireland is fortunate in that this significant phase of urban development coincided with a period of high standards in design and taste generally throughout Europe. Architecture, urban design, painting, and sculpture were all of social importance. The aesthetic character of towns was influenced by social conditions of the time. During the early nineteenth century, the population on the island was approaching eight million people. The great majority lived in the countryside, with pockets of extremely high density. The towns acted as service and administrative centers for this population, and so were dotted more or less evenly throughout the country. In a small town or village every building on the main street was a shop of some sort or another—butcher, draper, grocer, hardware, and, of course, the public house. Shops might provide three or more services in the same establishment. The classic example is the pub situated at the back of the grocery, which at the same time sells a little bit of hardware, drapery, and the local newspapers. When dropping in for a drink, one could also buy a shirt, a pair of boots, or a spade or a shovel.

Spacious streets and squares, influenced by Classical ideas in town planning, also facilitated the holding of fairs and the establishment of markets. This was also a time of administrative change. The new public buildings—churches, markets, courthouses, and halls—emphasized the administrative importance of the town. Towns were not only centers of commerce and administration, but were also, of course, living places: the shopkeeper living above his shop; the doctor or lawyer beside his rooms. This mixture of workplace and home, which influenced visual characteristics, can still be observed in the smaller towns and villages.

From the mid-nineteenth century onward, urban development continued on a more reduced scale. The great concentration of effort was now in Ulster, particularly the northeastern part, and this period has also left an interesting heritage, especially of industrial and commercial building. This relative lack of development—some small towns remained unchanged for a hundred years or more and until recently retained their Classical simplicity and charm—resulted in pleasantly proportioned facades, attractive shopfronts, fine public buildings, and perhaps most of all the physical attachment of buildings to their neighbors. This is an essential feature of old towns everywhere, particularly in the European tradition, and it is perhaps the most significant physical feature that distinguishes old settlements from their modern counterparts.

The essential element, therefore, of Irish town architecture is a Classical one, a dominant factor still despite many changes in recent years. A wide variety of buildings is to be found. They were influenced by the architectural fashions of the day, although the impact was shaped by local factors, such as topography, economic conditions, social attitudes, and building traditions. Because of Ireland's geographical location, architectural ideas and building techniques were often slow in arriving, but this does not necessarily reduce their significance. In many ways it adds to their interest. There are finely proportioned street houses, many of three or four stories, built for the professional classes, but now often used for offices in the cities and larger towns; smaller two-story and single-story houses, built for the artisan and skilled worker, still mainly in residential use and becoming quite fashionable to live in. Houses were usually built of brick in the cities; in the smaller towns, of local stone, plastered, and often brightly colored.

The public buildings—courthouses and markets, town halls, schools, and hospitals —embraced a wide range of styles, many indicating a comprehensive knowledge of Classical proportion and detail on the part of their designers and builders. Churches of different denominations reflected the various branches of Christianity. There are also fine Victorian public buildings, which usually exhibit a more diverse range of building styles. For example, many late-nineteenth-century Catholic churches, some of which are of cathedral-like proportions, even in relatively small towns, are built in a robust Gothic Revival style, a testimony to a new spirit of religious demonstration. For years their architectural and building qualities were underestimated and too many have been insensitively modernized to conform with new liturgical requirements.

Traditional shopfronts in Irish towns demonstrate the treatment of Classical details with a native freshness and vigor. Smaller shops may have simple columns made in timber, executed with a local interpretation, but, perhaps with all the more charm. The bigger shops have more ornate details, such as hand-carved Ionic or Corinthian columns, executed in stone by craftsmen, often working from pattern books. There is fine hand-painted lettering, executed with a distinctive flourish, aiming always at artistic expression more than ordinary craft. The lettering includes many alphabetical variations. In some districts it is possible to distinguish the trademark of a master craftsman who gives an individual flourish to certain letters. Lettering and signs frequently respect the architectural style of the building, and even the smallest letters can be read without any difficulty. Traditional shopfronts are indeed one of the glories of small-town architecture; they are now highly prized after many years of neglect.

An interesting visual feature of Irish towns is the marvelous and uninhibited use of strong color, particularly characteristic of towns in the Southwest. This is usually relieved by contrasting tones for the smaller details.

As in other countries, modern architecture was slow to come to terms with the discipline of building in existing towns. The earliest examples were brash and self-assertive and ignored the need to conform, and in the course of time there arose a general desire for buildings with which people could identify. The most recent modern buildings are more reticent and respectful of existing situations. The modern era is perhaps best exemplified by the flight to the suburbs. In approaching every town, one finds a variety of houses, garages, and factories, all individually built on separate sites: Cohesion and relationship are absent. These recent developments have been influenced by the dictates of the motor car and the availability of relatively cheap petrol, and the "urban sprawl" has continued far out into the countryside, perhaps under the impetus of the long-standing tradition of rural living, although now the owners are rarely engaged in rural occupations. The new houses all face toward the road, too often ignoring the site orientation, and the design frequently reflects foreign influences rather than traditional Irish methods of building. The fine visual distinction between town and countryside, still common to other European countries, is being eroded, and we have not yet conceived an acceptable aesthetic approach to building in the countryside. The aesthetic qualities of the old farm buildings have been seriously undervalued, because old images of poverty and backwardness die hard. But this is a topic for another essay. At the end we return to our towns.

It is difficult at this time, despite the many significant improvements in communications, to visualize a completely new life-style as an alternative to the traditional town. Man will always need the stimulus, which over the centuries he has derived from face-to-face contacts—a most significant aspect of urban living.

A major task, not only in Ireland but all over the world, is to make cities and towns more pleasant and safer places to live in. There are now some positive trends in this direction to suggest that we may now be on the threshold of another significant phase in urban civilization: the regeneration of our town centers as places to live rather than as merely commercial entities. Many urban-renewal schemes have been implemented that emphasize the advantages of living in town centers, with easier access to community and cultural facilities and better use of energy resources. They hold out the hope that at the end of the century, town centers will again be vital and interesting places—their traditional role over the centuries.

THE GIRDLE OF THE SUBURBS

BY HUGH LEONARD

Forty or so years ago, there was a popular comic song beloved of such music-hall entertainers as Jimmy O'Dea and Fred (Howayah!) Johnson, who delivered it in a sneeringly la-di-da accent and ended each verse with a shuddered "Thank heavens we live in Wrath-gawh!" You will not find "Wrath-gawh" on a Dublin street map. In normal speech it is Rathgar, where it was once supposed that the posh people lived—or rather, those beings who had pretensions to poshness but could not quite aspire to the grandeur of Ballsbridge, two miles down the road.

In those days, the suburbs clung tightly around the city like day-old chicks around the mother hen. Walk only a half mile beyond the sedate avenues of Victorian red brick and the mock-Georgian fanlights, and you came to green fields; the footpaths ended and the street lamps became distant pockmarks of yellow in the dark. The girdle of suburbs began with Ringsend on the Liffey's south bank, a working-class huddle of small, soot-blackened houses standing cheek-by-jowl with factories. Around the corner was Sandymount, and you were going up in the world: The houses still tipped their hats to you deferentially, but they had pocket-handkerchief gardens and front gates that squeaked with modest pride. Next came Ballsbridge with its embassies and elegance, the Horse and Spring shows, the discreet gardens and houses of "the quality."

Further inland along the arc were Donnybrook, Ranelagh, Rathmines, and Rathgar, from which the white of collar caught their trams to and from their offices in Merrion Square or on Earlsfort Terrace. In the evenings, they queued to see *Meet John Doe* or *Since You Went Away* at the Stella Picture House or the Kenilworth, or they sidled out for a furtive pint at Madigan's or Kiely's. The suburban pub was still a male preserve, a reef on which the stalwart husband and father could run aground and founder. On Sundays, the families went to the parks or the nearest seashore, or the trams would bear them out to the promenade and the brass band at far-off (six miles) Dun Laoghaire or the cliff walks at Howth to the north.

Furthest inland from the city were the new suburbs of Kimmage and Crumlin, fearsome jungles of pebble-dashed corporation dwellings where, you were told, inadvertent interlopers would never live to see the morrow's sun come up. On the North Side and across the river, the arc swung back toward the sea, through Phibsborough, Glasnevin, Marino, Fairview, and Clontarf, the circle now complete except for the thin segment of the Liffey cutting to its center.

I have written of these suburbs in the past tense, although they still survive, even if in many cases as an amorphous bed-sitterland, because of a phenomenon common to cities in other lands that has now overtaken Dublin and, come to that, Cork, Limerick, and Galway.

What happened may be summed up in a single word: wheels. Mr. Dunphy, in whose raincoat pocket bicycle clips jangled in 1950, was, ten years later, the owner of a Ford Consul or a Renault Dauphine. His friends were no longer of necessity Mr. Hanafin, who lived next door but one, or Mr. Minogue in Saint Angela's Terrace up the street, turn right, and it's facing you. Instead, he could now drive clear across the city and have a jar with Joe Delaney from the office, who lived off out in Raheny, a nice little housing estate, brand-new and with central heating, would you credit it? Makes a man think.

Mrs. Dunphy was meanwhile doing some thinking, too, and if there was a one-word reason in her case, it was "television." For the first time, she was seeing different homes, different life-styles, in which what to her had seemed inaccessible luxuries were taken for granted. She saw fitted kitchens, appliances, gardens, tree-lined avenues instead of terraces where one lived in next door's pocket, and she decided that she wanted her share.

The exodus began. New suburbs sprang up, some poor, some affluent, each one a testament to modern Irish architecture: Which is to say that each house was a mirror image of the one next door, and it faced in the same direction. What had been rural hamlets were swallowed up, buried in a maze of semidetacheds: L-shaped lounge, dinette, kitchen, four bedrooms, bathroom, garage. The tiny village pub with hard chairs and fly-flecked mirrors had perhaps a year of wild prosperity as the new housing estates grew; so, too, did the one and only shop, where you bought newspapers, light bulbs, milk, shoe polish, boiled ham, and detergents, all over the same counter. Then they were swept away, the corner store and the pub, by the shopping malls, the supermarkets, and the lounge bars, plush with velveteen, bright with chrome.

What I am saying is that the Irish suburb, superficially, at any rate, is no different from its brethren on the outskirts of Boston, Birmingham, Lyons, or Milan. It is smaller, of course, because Dublin is smaller, and it has an unkempt appearance. Between the garden gates and the avenue there is invariably a wide strip of grass, usually with saplings planted at intervals; and, because no one ever weeds or mows the grass or prunes the trees, the effect is that of Eden after the Fall. Still, the similarities are bound to be disillusioning for the visitor from overseas, who discovers that he has left one suburb to find another one pretty much like it.

There are differences, however, if one looks deep enough. I once acquired a mild notoriety for saying that I enjoyed visiting America because it was the only part of the world that had not become Americanized. In fact, I spoke in earnest. America exults in its space: a conurbation can spread for twenty miles and no harm done; whereas Ireland is 140 miles wide from coast to coast; already the Dublin suburbs have collided with Dun Laoghaire, which in turn is jostling Bray, twelve miles out. Towns are in danger of becoming entangled with towns, and so by foreign standards our suburbs are Lilliputs.

The new suburbs have become self-contained, villages in themselves. One does not have to be a graybeard to remember the pleasures of bygone Dublin at and after sundown: a stroll by the canal or through "the Green" and down Grafton Street, window-shopping. It was a city made for idlers. Now, the walkers are purposeful: They are on their way to a theater or a restaurant and there is no dawdling. The suburbanites have given over the city center to the young and restive, and while O'Connell Street after dark is by no means as fraught with possible perils as parts of Manhattan, the mood—engendered by the times—is sullen and destructive. Dublin by night is no longer pleasant.

The more affluent suburbs cling to the curve of the bay or high up against the foothills, with the mountains behind; the not so well-to-do live in between, and it is these who have adapted to a new kind of life-style with the effortlessness of a tadpole becoming a frog. The pub, for example, is no longer a sanctuary for an endangered male species: It has become a common ground where families may meet without the trouble of entertaining at home. The feminine influence is apparent: There are carpets on the floor, Formica on the tabletops, the lighting is muted, and there is the sound of Muzak dribbling through the ceilings. The noise level is earsplitting, and at weekends any suburban pub is so crowded as to suggest that a return visit by the Pope is imminent.

It would be cozy but untrue to say that underneath the sports jackets, the tailored denims, the suedes, and the Italian knitwear, the Irish have remained invincibly unchanged. Dublin suburbia, for example, has become a kind of melting pot. The true Dublinman (as opposed to a Dubliner, meaning one who merely lives there) is fiercely himself; he can and will recite a list of his forebears, all born within two miles of the Liffey quays; he has his own kind of humor and is fiercely disdainful of anyone hailing from the far side of Tallaght or Finglas. To him, country people who now live in Dublin are known by the derogatory term "culshies." The origin of the term is uncertain, but the "culshy" in his archetypal form is a country dweller with pretensions toward intelligence who works in the civil service or a bank or a similar institution where the entrance examination is all.

In spite of the one-time derision, the assimilation is now complete. A new kind of Dublinman has emerged. He lives in Ballinteer or Pine Valley. He speaks with an accent redolent of Cork or Mayo, but his children's speech is pure Dublinese. He works for Irish Life Assurance or Shell Oil or Dunlop. He drives a Volvo; his wife, trim and weight conscious, imperils hundreds of lives daily in a Mini or a Renault 5. He is fond of his pint after work, he is on his local residents' committee, he plays squash on Wednesdays, he goes to Crete or the Algarve each summer, and, for all his lip service to republicanism, his only real interests are his family and friends and outwitting the tax man.

And there is a kind of unease, of guilt. He grew up in a terrace house, or perhaps a cottage, where the family bathwater was boiled on a gas stove or the kitchen fire, where the milk curdled in the summer because there was no fridge, where back-breaking work made his mother old at forty. As a youth, he changed his shirts twice a week, and a torn jacket was a calamity. The word "lunch" was unknown. You ate dinner—"*your* dinner" or "*the* dinner," it was called—at one P.M., and "tea" was at six: bread and jam, or cheese, or, on Sundays, cold meat. Your horizons were the nearby streets, the picture house, school, and a balding field to play in. Except in high summer, you were never warm. Now, grown up and married, you inhabit a different world, one that your work-worn parents never knew, and deep inside you as you trot out to rent a movie on videotape or ask the barman to put ice in your Scotch, there is a quiet, gnawing sense of betrayal.

It accounts, perhaps, for the Irishman's contempt for "codology," meaning affectation. Tell someone that next year you are planning to go on a cruise, and the reply will be: "'Twas far from it you were reared!" It is at once a reminder and a warning not to forget your humble beginnings. The suburbanite's fear of seeming affected, of having gone "high-hat," is so pervading that he goes to the other extreme: He turns being natural into effeteness, he is ashamed of his hard-earned life.

My own town, Dalkey, was once a village; now, although ten miles from central Dublin, it is in effect a suburb. The fields and green spaces that marked its separateness from the city have been eaten up by housing developments. And yet, instead of merging into the sprawl, it has reinforced its identity as a place. It looks after its old; there is a youth club; it fiercely preserves its amenities against "improvements." In these respects, it is not unique among suburbs, but typical and, incidentally, an aberration: The New Irish have perversely learned to pull together.

The real victims of the sea change are the cities. Dublin has always been accorded the adjective "dirty," used in a fond sense; now, there is a sadness about it, as if its heart has gone elsewhere. It is bustling and cacophonous by day, but its night life is gone. The suburbs, in contrast, ring with folk groups and balladeers in the "singing" pubs; there is pub theater, where one need not wait with caked lips for the intermission for one's pint. The smart boutiques, specialty shops, and department stores have followed their customers out into what not many years ago were "the wilds."

And in the ubiquitous pub or over the fake log fire in the living room, when the all-seeing eye of the TV set has faded to a white spot, the exiles from "Wrath-gawh," Phibsborough, and Ballybough reminisce about the times when they were happier and poorer and grimier, when Dublin, for all its seediness, was its real self. The phrase "the good old days" is likely to crop up. Whenever it does in my own hearing, I remember an evening in Maryland when an actor, the late John McGiver, and I were reminiscing, and a young stagehand said: "I only hope that when I'm older I'll have stories like that to tell."

John looked at him sternly and, in his best professorial voice, said: "Hey man, *these* are the good old days!"

PAGE 121   *Kylemore Abbey, County Galway, since 1920 a Benedictine convent*

ABOVE   *Castle Ward. The Classical front of an eccentric mansion built between*
1762 and 1768 in two styles for Bernard Ward, later the first Lord Bangor.
He preferred the Classical idiom, his wife, the neo-Gothic.

*Beaulieu House, County Louth, built in the Dutch style (1660–67). It was
one of the first big houses in Ireland to be built without fortification.*

ABOVE *Muckross House, Killarney, County Kerry. Built in 1843, it now contains a folk museum.*

OPPOSITE, ABOVE *Glin Castle, County Limerick, seat of the Knights of Glin for 700 years*

OPPOSITE, BELOW LEFT *Portion of a painted plaster ceiling in Glin Castle,
probably done by Michael Stapleton about 1782*

OPPOSITE, BELOW RIGHT *At Glin Castle,
three important pieces of Irish eighteenth-century furniture:
a richly carved mahogany bureau bookcase of about 1765; at right, a walnut fiddle-back chair from
the 1730s; and, at left, a splat-back mahogany armchair made in mid-century*

PAGES 126 AND 127 *Irish vernacular architecture features
the use of strong colors in many attractive and contrasting combinations.
These examples are from various parts of the country.*

ABOVE *Mullaghmore, County Sligo*

128

ABOVE *The craft of thatching is being revived after coming close to extinction. A thatcher at work in County Clare*

LEFT *"Ni hé lá na gaoithe lá na scolb." (A windy day is bad for thatching.) Most Irish proverbs are deeply rooted in rural experience.*

ABOVE *Mural art on a derelict building, County Limerick*

LEFT *Weaver at Kilkenny Design Centre, creative focus
for many craft and design skills*

OPPOSITE *Craft shop, Bantry, County Cork*

OPPOSITE   *Clonfert Cathedral, County Galway, the thirteenth-century successor to the monastery founded by Saint Brendan in 558*

ABOVE LEFT   *Romanesque heads, Clonfert*

ABOVE RIGHT   *Romanesque doorway, Clonfert*

BELOW LEFT   *Modern stonework, Corcomroe Abbey, County Clare*

BELOW RIGHT   *The west high cross, Clonmacnoise, County Offaly. Clonmacnoise was founded by Saint Ciaran (Kieran) in 548. A scene on the high cross depicts the foundation.*

FURNISHED WITH THE LAUGHTER OF THE YEARS

BY DESMOND GUINNESS

The castles that stand as romantic ruins all over the country are regarded with affection today, an attitude very far from the awe in which they were once held. A tower house, for the local clan chief and his family, would often have a thatched hall beside it that was the center of life in times of peace. A curtain wall would enclose the bawn, into which cattle and sheep would be herded for safety, as cattle raiding was a regular occurrence. Conditions were primitive. Luke Gernon, an English visitor, wrote in 1620: "When you come to your bedchamber do not expect a canopy and curtains, the wild Irish have no candles on their tables. . . . What! Do I speak of tables? Indeed, they have no tables, but set their meat upon a bundle of grass and use the same grass as napkins to wipe their hands." For reasons of safety, the castle lasted in Ireland for far longer than was necessary elsewhere. The year 1641 saw a bloody rebellion, and soon after, the country was subjected to Cromwell's ruthless suppression.

Bunratty Castle was palatial in contrast to the numerous tower houses of the lesser gentry that abound in County Clare, and the O'Brien Earls of Thomond held court here in a manner that left a profound impression on the Papal Nuncio, Rinuccini. "In Italy there is nothing like the palace grounds of the Lord Thomond, nothing like its ponds and park with its three thousand head of deer," he wrote after a visit to Bunratty Castle in the seventeenth century.

In 1660 a remarkable house, Beaulieu, was built to the north of Drogheda. It is virtually unique in that it has never changed hands by purchase, although the property has more than once descended in the female line. The great hall, where family portraits gaze at each other across the shafts of sunlight, is one of the most peaceful and yet dramatic rooms in any Irish house, furnished as it is with the laughter of the years.

Mount Ievers Court, in County Clare, incorporates the family name in that of the house, as is so often found in Ireland. The Ievers family still lives here, hidden from the world down a long drive, as though in some remote and forgotten doll's house. It is a pre-Palladian house, with the accent on the steeply pitched roof and the giant chimney stacks, but it was built in 1732, ten years after the Palladian style had reached the eastern part of Ireland. A time lag in architectural styles existed between the more cosmopolitan East and the West of Ireland. As early as 1722, a "correct" Palladian house was built near Dublin, which was destined to become, as headquarters of the Irish Georgian Society, the first country house in the vicinity of the capital to open its doors to visitors. This house, Castletown, in Celbridge, County Kildare, was built for a powerful politician, William Conolly, who was Speaker of the House of Commons in the Dublin Parliament and was always known as "Speaker" Conolly. The architect was Alessandro Galilei, an Italian whose only Irish creation it was. Castletown was the first Palladian house in Ireland; it is also still the largest, and to some tastes it is the most beautiful. The facade consists of a vast central block, like an Italian town palace, with wings on either side, joined by curved colonnades that extend forward to greet the visitor in a gesture of welcome.

The first architect to settle in Ireland and establish the Palladian style was a German, Richard Castle, who lived in Ireland from 1728 until he died in 1752. He built canals and public buildings as well as country houses and had a huge practice, but little is known of his origins and, as nothing has yet been attributed to him outside Ireland, his name is not as well known as it deserves to be.

One of Castle's most famous houses, on account of the drama of its natural setting, is Powerscourt, County Wicklow, built in 1731 and ravaged by fire in 1974. Its frontage has the basic strength and simplicity always to be found in his work. Russborough, County Wicklow, also designed by Castle and built from 1741 onward, has a facade of no less than seven hundred feet, and stands in rolling countryside facing the Wicklow Mountains across a vast man-made expanse of water. Utilitarian yards are formed on either side, which serve to lengthen the front and make it more imposing. The curved colonnades and wings create a forecourt of great elegance, for all the world like a miniature eighteenth-century parade ground.

Not by any means were all of the country seats in Ireland put up by architects: The lesser gentry were anxious to emulate their more sophisticated neighbors and provide themselves with the usual list of "necessities." These included a lake or a "sheet of water," a belt of beech trees, a walled garden, and a temple or grotto. The garden was not infrequently a longish walk from the house, shut up in its gray stone walls, lined in brick to ripen the fruit, and firmly locked on Sundays. The house might have been designed by the person who commissioned it; he would hand over to a local builder his sketches, inspired by something he had admired on a visit abroad, or culled from some out-of-date building pattern book. These amateurish creations were often old-fashioned when they were built and the Classical motifs misemployed, giving an appearance of naiveté.

The Irish house is sometimes named after the family that built it: for instance, Castle Ward and Mount Ievers Court. Bessborough, County Kilkenny, was named for Elizabeth Ponsonby, and Dollymount for a wife called Dolly. This was altered by the grandson to Delamont, just as Mount Tally-Ho was later to become Montalto. Mount Falcon, County Mayo, was the seat of the Faulkner family and the house is a pun on the family name.

The great Dublin town houses, such as Leinster, Charlemont, and Aldborough, were invariably named after their owners. They were built of stone, and they stand out against the terraces of faded red brick, washed by years of Irish weather to a magical pink of startling beauty. By far the largest is Leinster House, now the seat of Dáil Éireann (the Irish Parliament), a stone town palace of gigantic proportions designed by Richard Castle in 1745. Only one of Dublin's great town houses is still inhabited as was the original intention, and it is among the finest of them all: the Provost of Trinity College is indeed to be envied for the splendor of his lodgings, designed for entertaining with dignity and style. The great saloon on the upper floor stretches the entire width of the house.

Like Dublin, the provincial towns had their "season," and it was not uncommon for a house to be kept up in (say) Limerick or Galway as well as in the capital, where the social life centered around Parliament and the court of the British viceroy.

By 1762 taste, among those able to afford to build a country seat, was beginning to change. Horace Walpole had built Strawberry Hill outside London in the Gothic Revival style and the tide was beginning to turn in this direction. Mr. Bernard and Lady Anne Ward, it is said, could not agree as to the design of their new house in County Down. He wanted it to be Classical and she wanted it Gothic. The result was an architectural and matrimonial compromise that is surely unique. One front is Classical in style, and the other is Gothic; obviously, the rooms on "his" side of the house have Classical interiors and on "her" side Gothic pendants hang from the ceilings and the marble mantels are in the Gothic taste. A local wit remarked that the identity of the architect was "not known and best forgotten." Thus by the end of the Georgian period the wheel of fashion had turned full circle: In 1700 the house evolved from the castle; by 1800 the reverse had happened—the castle evolving from the house. Was it perhaps that people were bored with the sameness of the Classical house? Why else did they clamor to evoke the spirit of medieval times, with mock battlements and turrets, suits of armor and pyramids of cannonballs?

Tullynally Castle in County Westmeath was a Classical house built for the Pakenhams about 1760. In 1806 a mantle of Gothic was flung over it, and no trace of the original house can be seen, as far as the exterior is concerned. The seat to this day of the Earls of Longford, Tullynally Castle was treated to its "improvements" shortly after the Act of Union, in 1801, when the Dublin Parliament was abolished and direct rule from Westminster was imposed. This resulted in fashion deserting Dublin for London. Dublin became a provincial backwater; the great town houses were given up by their noble owners and more attention was paid to the country seat.

Fortunately for posterity, family pride has always been one of the besetting sins of the Anglo–Irish. Families were ruined attempting to outdo their neighbors. On occasion sheds for horses and cattle were designed to look like part of the house, in order that it should appear to be larger than it in fact was. The grandest gates—gates that would not be out of place in a public park—would sometimes lead to quite modest-sized houses so as to impress the passerby. The gate lodge was occasionally placed on the far side of the road from the driveway to demonstrate that the land on that side of the road also belonged to the estate.

The potato famine of 1845–51 brought about an end to country-house building or "improvement." The Victorian era saw a slowing down of private architectural commissions, although the railway age produced some memorable public buildings.

In the eighteenth century, the park, or "demesne," had been chosen for its beauty rather than for its good farming qualities. Tenant farms provided the income that was spent on embellishing the demesne with trees, lakes, and buildings, all in harmony with one another. In 1903 the Wyndham Act put an end to the system, and tenanted land was taken from the landlords of Ireland in exchange for financial compensation. Selling land had always been a last resort; spending Government bonds came easily. The great house and its demesne were left, stranded high and dry like a head without a body to support it. In Dublin the town houses became clubs, offices, or worse; their unbelievably fine and varied interiors have survived many vicissitudes, and access is often granted on request.

It is often only the gates, piercing the crumbling demesne walls, that are left to recall that there was once a great house here, a garden, a park, a library of books, and a family growing up wedded to the magic of the place and very proud of it.

The present century has seen an endless catalogue of burnings and unroofings, so that the houses and castles that remain in Ireland are particularly to be cherished. Their future may well lie in tourism. They tell the visitor so much of the country's past, of her customs, art, and artifacts; if and when the State comes to realize their potential as a tourist attraction their future will cease to be in jeopardy.

ORIGINALITY AND BRAVURA

BY THE KNIGHT OF GLIN

The three-thousand-year period from roughly 1500 B.C. to A.D. 1500 saw the flowering of early Irish art—the dazzling metalwork of torque and shrine, the subtle intricacies of interlace and spiral on the manuscript page, priceless artifacts such as the Book of Kells, the Ardagh Chalice, the Tara Brooch, and the Shrine of Saint Patrick's Bell, which take their triumphant place in the forefront of the art of the world.

With the coming of the Middle Ages and the Norman invasion Irish art suffered a decline in originality, and very few examples of woodwork, ceramics, and textiles predating the seventeenth century have survived. A more peaceable atmosphere was, however, to bring an economic recovery and a new flowering, and in the eighteenth century Dublin became the center for luxury crafts, many of them, such as woodcarving, plasterwork and ironwork, associated with the great spate of building that began after the Williamite wars. The richer classes had the need for fine silverware, furniture, ceramics, glass, textiles, and bookbinding and, as with the decorative arts of colonial America, Ireland's vocabulary of ornament, in spite of belonging to the English and Western European tradition, takes on a local flavor and frequently exhibits an idiosyncratic and individual twist. In this purely personal survey I have dealt mainly with the eighteenth century and have tended to highlight this individual quality, concentrating on the whims and differences that we find in the craftsmanship of the period rather than on the conventional styles that echo English idioms.

The interior of the late-seventeenth-century house, both in town and country, was usually wainscoted in deal, and this paneling was often painted in very surprisingly bright colors, such as duck-egg blue, reds, and greens. Carving was concentrated around the staircase and chimneypiece and was often extremely elaborate, as in the case of the over-doors in the great hall at Beaulieu, County Louth, or the banisters and frieze of the Damer House staircase in Roscrea, County Tipperary.

The incredibly elaborate Caroline oak staircase formerly at Eyrecourt Castle, County Galway, with its riot of acanthus, grotesque masks, and elaborate strapwork, may well have been imported from Holland; Dutch influence is to be found in Dublin craftsmanship, but it was a family of French carvers, the Tabarys, who created the superb oak carving of the altarpiece and altar table at Sir William Robinson's Royal Hospital, Kilmainham. The swagged fruit and flowers, trophies, palm-tree fronds, and cherubs show a clearness and sureness of touch unequaled until then in Irish woodwork. The Tabarys' carving influenced the work at Beaulieu and in the organ case of Saint Mary's Church, Dublin (1702). Fine quality architectural woodwork flourished in the interiors of the great Dublin town palaces in Henrietta Street and other houses on the north side of the city. Mahogany became a new import in the late 1730s and the carved mahogany staircase and magnificent pedimented doors at Richard Castle's famous country house, Russborough, in County Wicklow, brilliantly exhibits the superlative quality of Irish carving of this period.

Pine paneling was replaced by stucco in the early to mid-eighteenth century, and the influence of the English Palladians and William Kent's tabernacle frames and compartmented ceilings can be found in Sir Edward Lovett Pearce's interiors at numbers 9 and 10 Henrietta Street, Dublin, or at Bellamont Forest, his porticoed villa in County Cavan. The German Richard Castle, who succeeded to his practice, carried on this robust early Georgian decoration in many of his own Palladian houses. The plaster decoration at Russborough —and at Carton and Castletown in County Kildare—contains the work of the Francini brothers, *stuccatori* from Ticino in the Italian area of Switzerland, who came from England to Ireland in the 1730s. The Carton dining room (now the saloon) of 1739 is their finest work, two stories high and with its Baroque coved ceiling peopled by mythological figures and plump *putti* playing on festoons of leaves while Jove hurls his thunderbolts at us from the central panel. French Rococo influence is also very strong in mid-century Dublin, and the Rotunda Hospital Chapel, decorated by Barthèlemy Cramillion, is a typical *tour de force*.

The high point of this style is found in the work of the Dublin-born Robert West, with his marvelous flights of birds, trophies of musical instruments, and Rococo swirling curls and flourishes as seen in 20 Dominick Street, 20 Parnell Square, and Newman House in

Dublin. The fantasy of this superb Rococo plaster was soon, however, to be superseded by the geometric Neoclassical interiors of Michael Stapleton, who popularized the Robert Adam and James Wyatt styles. All over Ireland houses were extravagantly decorated in this newly fashionable "antique" taste reflecting the Roman plasterwork found at the recent excavations at Pompeii and Herculaneum. The hall ceiling at Glin Castle, County Limerick, is a fine example and survives with its original pastel coloring. It is probably by Stapleton or one of his school.

In the latter part of the seventeenth and early eighteenth centuries domestic furniture —oak, walnut, and japanned pieces—closely reflected that produced in England, and documented pieces such as Tabary's altar table at Kilmainham are a rarity. There is a group of extremely elaborate and quirkish inlaid walnut writing cabinets which show, on the other hand, considerable Dutch influence and are remarkable for their inlaid marquetry decoration. One of these is now on show at Florence Court, County Fermanagh. The Kentian Baroque Irish mahogany furniture also has a style very much its own and portrays all kinds of oddities in its carved ornament—heavy paw feet, a curious bulging acanthus hock, birdlife, and animal masks—which give it a life of its own. One can easily imagine these splendid sideboards and bureau cabinets moving with low grunts around the floor! By no means was all the furniture so elaborate, and a plainer and very elegant style also existed: neat little tea tables, card and gaming tables, and fiddleback chairs with flat stretchers, all echoing Hogarth's cursive "line of beauty." This furniture is in some cases extremely similar to contemporary American examples, particularly those from Philadelphia.

The craft of bookbinding flourished, achieving its greatest freedom between 1740 and 1765. Dublin bindings of the period are even more original than the city's Rococo ceilings. An unknown genius, known to scholars as "Parliamentary Binder B" (whose bindings for the *Journals of the House of Lords* are now, alas, destroyed), invented "a way of tooling the leather so as to give the impression of the surfaces of feathers, catching the light like a cornfield under wind," as Maurice Craig has described them. These incredible bindings were quite unique, and the care lavished on these transactions of Parliament indicates how much the members thought of themselves. The same proliferation of ornament can be seen in the grandiosely illuminated Irish Peerage patents, which are far more ostentatious than those provided by the English College of Arms. This love of display would seem characteristic of Ireland's Ascendancy and it runs through many of the decorative arts, from the massive, overcarved mahogany side tables already mentioned to the highly elaborate interiors of Dublin houses which are, by contrast, so reticent and uniform on the outside.

The mahogany status-symbol side table was made to display a profusion of plate, and Irish eighteenth-century silver is probably the best known and highly sought after item in the field of Irish decorative arts. The Goldsmiths' Company had been founded in Dublin in 1637, and its tradition of assay marks continues to this day. Silver, like furniture, is relatively plain until about 1740. It was not particularly innovatory or imaginative, with the occasional exception such as the extraordinary swan-necked wine cistern of 1715 by John Hamilton, now in the Ulster Museum. A very Irish silver type, also associated with drinking, is the two-handled cup with harp-shaped handles, which was used on festive occasions for drinking toasts and was often given as a prize at race meetings. Subsequent celebrations would certainly have seen many a steaming hot bowl of whiskey punch, inevitably placed on a dish ring, which acted as a coaster to protect the polished mahogany table. An example by John Lloyd, of about 1770, in the National Museum in Dublin, shows typical, very fine Rococo decoration with birds, festoons, and fruit and flowers very akin to Dublin Rococo ceilings and even to the decoration on furniture.

The interrelation between the various arts and the sophistication of design in Ireland at this time owes much to the progressive training that Irish craftsmen could obtain free at the Dublin Society drawing school under the tutelage of the French-educated masters Robert West and James Manin. Irish silver is often humorously chased in repoussé, with farmyard scenes or amusing subjects such as that on the three-footed sugar bowl by Matthew West in the National Museum, which depicts a milkmaid being spied upon by an amorous shepherd peeping around a traditional Irish round tower. Such rural scenes even appear on mantelpiece plaques carved in marble and sometimes form an incongruous contrast to the staid lines of the mantelpieces themselves. Neoclassicism was soon to ban such frivolity, and by the 1780s the newly elegant shapes were highlighted by chiseled, bright-cut engraving on everything from silver spoon to silver teapot. This engraving was frequently carried out by the same craftsmen who cut the elaborate metal plates for contemporary book illustration, again demonstrating the interconnection between the various branches of the art of decoration. The shimmering effect produced by bright-cut silver on a candlelit table was particularly attractive; and engraved glass shares this sparkling, iridescent quality.

Lead glass had been manufactured in Dublin since the late seventeenth century but it was not until the mid-eighteenth century that anything very memorable was made. The great period of Irish glass was to come after 1780, when the new laws on Irish free trade, combined with the duty imposed on imported glass, encouraged the industry and even attracted English glassmakers to Ireland. The characteristic heavy weight and deep ornamentation date from this time, and glass was exported all over the world from Dublin, Cork, Waterford, and Belfast. Charmingly engraved decanters, diamond-cut glasses, turnover-rim fruit bowls, and little piggins for butter are common enough, but perhaps the most original production was the branched chandelier, made to hang in front of an oval wall mirror decorated around the edge with glass "jewels" of various colors. These are a uniquely Irish feature.

Tin-glazed earthenware, or delft, enjoyed a brief period of splendor when, under the encouragement of the Dublin Society, Captain Henry Delamain took over an existing factory in 1753 and produced a wide variety of wares such as round and octagonal plates, tureens, bowls, pierced baskets, and the occasional wine fountain. This delft was often decorated with Italianate landscapes traditionally attributed to Peter Shee, a self-taught painter working in the factory. They clearly show the influence of the contemporary Dublin artist John Butts, particularly in their pudgy little figures. Butts was well known for faking and copying Flemish seventeenth-century paintings and this is where these little scenes ultimately derive from.

Irish textile production is overshadowed by lace, although a few tapestries were made in the late seventeenth century and those of Jan de Beaver are well known. Linen printing from copperplates produced highly sophisticated *toile de Jouy* prints by Robinson of Ballsbridge and Dixon of Leixlip.

Other than in the world of silver, the names of Irish craftsmen can rarely be associated with the objects they produced, though some decorated and engraved brass grates bear signatures, and hall lanterns occasionally have a name on them. At Birr Castle, County Offaly, the Dublin-made engraved brass grate by Jas. Jon. Clarke, Aston Quay, is bow-fronted and complete with draped stage curtains—a theatrical touch that somehow sums up the originality and bravura so often encountered in Ireland's decorative arts.

THE SWING OF THE PENDULUM

BY BRIAN FALLON

It is usual to regard the Irish as a literary race and virtually nothing else; the Irish Literary Revival has completely overshadowed the Irish artists of the time and those since. Perhaps the only Irish artist of the twentieth century whom the average cultured person could name is Jack B. Yeats, and even that is mainly because of the vastly greater fame of his poet brother. How often one hears the remark that Ireland has no painters to put beside her best writers!

In fact she has, and leaving out altogether the Golden Age of Celtic monasticism, the Book of Kells, *et al*, Irish art has a very respectable history over the last century and a half. Irish Romantics such as William Mulready (1786–1863) and Francis Danby (1793–1861) belong more to the history of English than of Irish art, but that is largely because London offered greater scope for their ambitions and talents. A little later Daniel Maclise (1806–1870), who was born in Cork, became the leading "history" painter of the early Victorian era and one of the fathers of the Pre-Raphaelite movement. These men were not solely an Anglo–Irish phenomenon—they belong in fact to the history of European Romanticism: Maclise was much influenced by German art and, in turn, his work was known and respected on the Continent, while Danby was admired in France. Maclise, in many ways, is the painterly equivalent of Thomas Moore, whose *Melodies* he illustrated, and he was close personally to Dickens, who gave his funeral oration.

It will have been noticed, however, that the "exile" theme is ominously present in the lives of all these men. Nineteenth-century Ireland did produce artists of stature, but it was too narrow and provincial a setting to keep them at home for long.

The age of the Literary Revival was—a fact rarely appreciated—a very lively age in painting, though again there was the ominous tendency for the artists to emigrate, since the commissions and recognition still lay abroad. The reputation of John Butler Yeats (1839–1922) has been overshadowed by those of his sons, but he was probably the finest portraitist of his day in the English-speaking world, with the exception of Sargent at his rare best. Yeats was in fact the portraitist of the Irish writers and intelligentsia of a whole epoch—of Synge, of George Moore, of his own poet son, of Douglas Hyde and A.E. (George Russell)—and a deeply sensitive and sympathetic one, with a kind of Old-Masterish ability to get at the core of his sitters and "humanize" them without any loss of intellectual strength. Yet he was forced, when an old man, to emigrate to America and die there, because he could not compete either for speed or surface brilliance with the much younger William Orpen (1878–1931), a social and artistic figure of immense panache who won a European reputation in his day. Orpen spent most of his maturity in London and Paris and was one of Britain's official artists in the First World War, painting that most fateful event, the signing of the Versailles Treaty. Even before his death his Edwardian bravura seemed dated, and nobody can defend him today against the many (highly priced) potboilers he turned out; but a well-chosen centenary exhibition in the National Gallery of Ireland showed how unanswerably gifted he was at his best.

Orpen was rivaled, both in reputation and in bravura, by Sir John Lavery (1856–1941), an Ulsterman who virtually grew up in Scotland and became a leading figure in the once-famous Glasgow School, which is now being revived. Like Orpen he became a too-fashionable portraitist, like him too he was a war artist—but unlike him, he came back to Ireland in his later years, and his beautiful American wife (his second), Hazel, played a certain role in the negotiations for the Irish Treaty. Lavery did most of his best work early in his career, and there is nothing specifically Irish about it; he was thoroughly eclectic and cosmopolitan in style and outlook. As a young man he painted at Grez-sur-Loing, one of the centers of *pleinairisme,* and his works of that time have an atmospheric delicacy and a technical finesse that are often missing later. For instance, his Bridge at Grez series are among the most beautiful pictures produced in that period, when the crossing of Barbizon nature lyricism with the French academic tradition gave rise to a style that formed a more conservative parallel to the Impressionists.

Barbizon was the real nursery of the art of Nathaniel Hone (1831–1917), one of the three or four best Irish painters of any age, though any kind of international recognition has been very slow to come his way. After his French training he settled at Malahide, on the coast near Dublin, and became as much a painter of that region as Constable had been of Suffolk. The juxtaposition of these names is not made at random, since he and Constable have a lot in common, and the French landscapists from whom Hone learned were far more the legitimate progeny of Constable than were the English painters of eighty years after his death. Hone had his limitations—particularly in his color, which is often dour and lowering, almost monochrome, and gives many of his pictures (he had a big output) a certain sameness. Yet at his best he has a breadth and sheer power that make him stand out even in very high company, and he had a remarkable ability to set down the essentials of a landscape without being sidetracked into anything but the barest essences. There is little imagination in the usual sense, in fact very little invention even, but confronted by one of his big sky-and-land-and-sea canvases, you are held straightaway by the powerful unity of mood, the refusal to prettify, the born painter's seemingly effortless ability to make so much out of so little. Here, you might say, is a European landscapist in the great tradition that stretches back through the Barbizon artists, through Constable, back to Ruysdael and Wouwerman.

The very orthodox but sensitive style of Walter Osborne (1859–1904) is a good deal more domesticated and *intimiste* than Hone's brooding panoramas; in fact, Osborne shines (literally) in the areas where Hone is weakest. The two men were friends, both Anglo–Irish gentlemen with a Continental training. Osborne is a very versatile artist, good at landscape, at portraiture (particularly of women), but probably best of all in scenes of luminous, refined domestic intimacy. His light-flecked brushwork suggests Impressionism, but in fact Osborne was a late *pleinairiste* who never quite forsook the warm shadows of the nineteenth-century academics and Realists for the blue-gray tones of the Impressionists. He seems to me a finer painter than Sickert or Steer, or indeed almost any of his English contemporaries, but outside Ireland, how many people have heard of him? Perhaps his inclusion in the huge exhibition of Post-Impressionism in London in the winter of 1979–80 will do something to redress the balance.

Another Irish (or Anglo–Irish) artist featured in that exhibition was the enigmatic Roderic O'Conor (1860–1940), who lived most of his life in France and was one of Gauguin's closest associates in Pont-Aven. (A large O'Conor exhibition is being organized for Belfast and Dublin, which will allow us to assess him more properly than has been possible to do so far.) Obscure in his lifetime, he has been discovered in the last quarter-century (a picture by him hangs in the Tate Gallery in London), and he will probably furnish potential biographers with materials for a very interesting life. O'Conor's changes of style are disconcerting—he painted like Gauguin, like Monet, like Renoir, like a kind of proto-Fauve, and also produced pictures in a perfectly conventional late-Realist manner. Perhaps the still lifes and flower pieces are ultimately his best things, and in these he shows himself a sensitive, traditional Intimist in what might be called the Franco–Irish style. Big claims are made for him, and the best of his output does justify them, but his admirers must shut their eyes to a large amount of curiously weak and undistinguished work, no better than that of two hundred (at least) other painters of the time. O'Conor's closest heir in the Franco–Irish line is William J. Leech (1881–1968), who painted in Brittany around the turn of the century but lived most of his long life in England.

It goes without saying that almost without exception, the artists I have mentioned have been Anglo–Irish and Protestant—like most of the figures of the Literary Revival. The reason is obvious enough; they represented the cultured, educated middle and upper-middle class, who could afford foreign study, often had private incomes, and could paint away even if they did not sell (Hone sold comparatively little in his lifetime, O'Conor hardly anything at all). With the coming of independence there was the inevitable sociocultural crisis in Irish art, even if it was not immediate or obvious. The new Free State looked for an official iconography that could not be satisfied by the old imagery of Irish wolfhounds, Celtic scrollwork and crosses, and the like, but in painting needed something more socially relevant.

As a result, an entire school of artists arose who painted the West of Ireland landscape and its people—cottagers, turf cutters, fishermen, all unmistakably "native" subjects. The best of them was Paul Henry (1876–1958), the son of a Belfast clergyman, who studied in Paris and absorbed not only late Realism but something from Cézanne and Seurat. Henry at his best is a solid, serious artist with a gift for simplifying landscape into stark, yet subtle, patterns of bog and sky and water, and for a certain kind of monumental figure painting that goes back to the early Van Gogh, and ultimately to Millet. His later work fell off sadly into staleness and lame repetition, but Henry is the virtual creator of the Western landscape; one might say he has created our whole image of that region, which quickly became such a stereotype in the hands of his followers, and even in his own at the end.

Henry's virtual reign over Irish painting was shared by Jack B. Yeats (1871–1957), and together they were a kind of duumvirate, seen by their own age as complementary units rather than rivals. Today Henry has shrunk to a local reputation, while Jack B. Yeats is probably the only Irish artist whose name has traveled at all far. Yeats was rather a late starter—his early work is mostly watercolor and black-and-white illustration, and up to the late 1920s it was largely "picturesque" in appeal. Tinkers, fairs, West of Ireland sights, Dublin street scenes, make up his typical subject matter. The work of this early period often has great zest and a very individual personality, and many find it complete in its own right, but Yeats was the type of "loner" artist who goes his own way, indifferent or oblivious to fashion, and develops late and in his own ultrapersonal, even eccentric, way.

Where to place Jack Yeats, and with whom can one compare him? The later work resembles European Expressionism, and in fact certain shrewd and knowing critics believe that Kokoschka—who knew Yeats personally—took more than a hint or two from him. But the comparison is shallow; Yeats has no real ancestry in Van Gogh, or Munch, or Gauguin. He does not even seem aware of Cézanne, or indeed of any Continental artist later than Daumier (who had a pronounced influence on Irish painters at the turn of the century, including Henry). He seems, in fact, an entirely isolated figure, owing little or nothing to the huge revolutions that, in his lifetime, were reshaping European painting. Yet the paradox is that he is still—in his mature work, that is—entirely modern; there is nothing in a late Yeats that is at all provincial or anachronistic. (It could even be argued that the freedom of brushwork and color in his very late work parallels or anticipates Abstract Expressionism, which almost certainly he would have dismissed as the work of chancy daubers and/or charlatans, even lunatics.)

Yeats was a genuine visionary, but one with his feet on the muddy ground of Irish life and his eye on the ordinary and everyday. The "folk" quality in his work is never forced and self-conscious, as it usually is in the writings of his elder brother, because both as a man and as an artist he possessed the common touch. He is at once a very subtle, even esoteric, artist and a "popular" painter whose work is easily accessible even to people who otherwise care little for art. He is, in short, Ireland's national painter and one of the few cases in which the word "national" does not imply something self-limiting, self-conscious, backward-looking. That is to say, he is both intensely Irish and utterly European.

Though a good "mixer," humorous and unspoiled, with none of the pomp-and-circumstance manner of his elder brother, Yeats was too private a man and too individualistic as an artist to found a school, or even to have followers in any literal meaning of the term. "Official" modernism in Ireland might be said to have begun with the founding in Dublin in 1943 of the Irish Exhibition of Living Art, the prime movers of which were two French-trained artists, Mainie Jellett and Evie Hone (1894–1955). Their modernism was the rather watered-down Cubism of Lhote and Gleizes, which gave rise to a style of painting with more prettiness than power. Evie Hone's reputation probably will rest on her stained glass; Mainie Jellett's late religious pictures, in a kind of Cubo-Futurist manner, have their admirers but belong to their period. Nevertheless, the IELA did form a nexus for a talented generation of artists in reaction against the academic camp—the latter largely recruited from the followers and pupils of Orpen, whose teaching and electric personality continued to dominate art in Dublin long after his departure overseas, and even after his death.

Artists such as Norah McGuinness (1903–1980), George Campbell (1917–1979), and the English-born Nevill Johnson (born 1911) continued this Irish Cubist tradition according to their own very individual temperaments. Colin Middleton (1910–1983), a Northern Irish artist, shows at various times the influence of Surrealism, Expressionism, and Ben Nicholson-style abstraction, yet he had a core of personality strong enough to survive all this. Two stronger personalities are Nano Reid (1903–1981) and Patrick Collins (born 1910), both of whom have absorbed Jack Yeats's very special balance of fantasy and earthiness. As painters they are rather hit-and-miss, but with a genuinely "Celtic" quality of imagination that is innate and unforced, with nothing of the made-to-order nationalism of the Free State artists. Nano Reid in her late work is curiously close at times to certain Action painters, such as Philip Guston, while Collins's cloudy, suggestive, half-buried imagery is that of a poet in paint, eloquent but untranslatable.

This Celtic ambience haunts the very original work of Tony O'Malley (born 1913), who has worked for much of his career in Cornwall and was close personally to many of the abstract and semiabstract painters of the St. Ives School. A more suavely cosmopolitan note is supplied by Louis le Brocquy (born 1916), one of the many painters who in the 1940s and 1950s reflected the influence of middle-period Picasso, and who seems as much at home in France and England as he does in his homeland. Le Brocquy is something of an eclectic: highly polished, a master of many styles and of many media (his tapestries are among his best works, and he has brilliantly illustrated in black and white Thomas Kinsella's translation of the old Gaelic epic the *Táin*).

The generation—or rather two generations—that has emerged since the war is too diverse to discuss in any detail here. Reacting against the chauvinism of thirty years ago, the younger artists are often aggressively "international," but it is far from certain that this will be the last swing of the pendulum.

A VIGOROUS RENEWAL

BY JUSTIN KEATING

Ireland was Britain's first colony, and Britain was the first country where the Industrial Revolution was accomplished. But far from producing a uniform social history over both islands, the enormous progress in manufacturing industry over the last few centuries left parts of Ireland extremely underdeveloped. Irish industries suffered severely in the circumstances of free trade with a much stronger partner, especially after the Act of Union in 1801. This very lack of development, however, while working to the detriment of most sectors of Irish life, benefited the crafts. When people were poor and transportation was difficult and dear, each community preserved all the traditional skills, not simply those of the stonemason, the blacksmith, and the woodworker, but those of the weaver, lacemaker, handknitter, basketmaker, and thatcher as well.

Their work was not respected as craft and has been little collected or preserved. The fashionable thing, when it came to furnishing a house, was to own the product of manufacturing industry. The new mass-produced objects were infinitely inferior in design and quality, but it was part of the ethos of the time that we lost a sense of the worth of what was indigenous and traditional. The process was not confined to Ireland; it was happening all over the industrializing world. It was our lack of modernity that saved some remnants of our crafts. But we also lacked an awareness of the historical and cultural value of these traditional objects. Great collections of handicraft objects began to be assembled in northern Europe almost one hundred years ago, but, to our shame, to this day we have no Museum of Folk Life, though there exists a fine collection that is not yet displayed.

We did have some survivors: the weavers and knitters along the West Coast, the linen in what is now Northern Ireland, pottery in places like Belleek in County Fermanagh and Carley's Bridge in Wexford, basketwork quite widely, but now surviving in only a few places like Carrick-on-Suir. The great days of Irish glass were over by the end of the first quarter of the nineteenth century. Irish silversmiths continued an unbroken tradition, but in the cities and for the rich. At its best, Irish silver was an artistic achievement of enormous proportions. Lacemaking had diminished from a large-scale operation with a worldwide reputation to a shadow, struck down, as were so many crafts, by the rise of the machine.

Almost a century ago, spearheaded by some remarkable writers, the arts in Ireland began a vigorous renewal. The literary revival was the precursor, almost the herald of a national revival that culminated in the establishment of a new state over sixty years ago. But in this upsurge of the arts there was a striking imbalance, which continued after independence. All the verbal arts were important: Plays, poetry, and novels appeared in enormous quantity and won a well-deserved reputation throughout the world. Vigorous efforts and high expenditure were devoted to reviving the Irish language and to collecting folklore and folk music. There was some progress in painting and sculpture, but, one may say bluntly, none in architecture or graphic design. And the crafts—unrespected, unnoticed, and uncared-for—languished. So it remained until the last fifteen years or so.

Of course there were honorable exceptions. But the philistine mass of the newly prosperous strove to make their suburban homes into replicas of the wastelands that were growing up in neighboring Britain. And later, Scandinavian-modern became trendy for the better-off. But since there was little interest in or market for traditional Irish crafts there was no vitality or growth in the craft sector. A number of voluntary organizations, however, strove nobly against the tide. Some extraordinary work done by the Dun Emer Guild is to be seen in the National Museum. The Royal Dublin Society has for two hundred and fifty years been unremitting in its efforts to improve all aspects of the quality of Irish life, crafts included. The Irish Countrywomen's Association and a few other voluntary organizations throughout the country did brave work—against the prevailing mood. In retrospect it seems hard to believe, but the Irish Crafts Council was only formed in the early 1970s, and it received no state aid whatsoever until a few years ago.

After the neglect and indifference of the public during the first half of the century, it is hard to determine the moment when the tide turned. But it did. It seems to me that in quality and intensity the crafts in Ireland now are really remarkable, and judging by the rate of improvement from year to year, the best is yet to be.

A number of state agencies have played a benevolent role. Córas Tráchtála (the Irish Export Board) was responsible for setting up the Kilkenny Design Workshops, whose mandate is much wider than the craft sector. The remarkable Kilkenny Shop in Dublin and its parent in Kilkenny give a breathtaking general impression of the range and quality of Irish craftwork. Bord Fáilte (the Irish Tourist Board) produces a very useful guide that enables the visitor to find not only craft shops but individual craftspersons, in all disciplines, all over the country. The Industrial Development Authority and its sister, the Shannon Development Company, have taken important initiatives in establishing craft centers where clusters of workshops house different disciplines. These extend from Marlay, near Dublin, to as far west as the beautiful Roundstone Centre in Connemara, and they provide welcome surroundings and growth potential for the artist/craftsman.

The new Irish craftsworkers demonstrate a change that is taking place everywhere in the craft world. The craftsworker used to practice a skill, handed down from generation to generation, often in an out-of-the-way part of the country. The craft was learned on the spot, and the only training was apprenticeship to a master craftsman. Now, everywhere in Ireland, we are seeing the rise of the artist/craftsman, often people with an art school background. They make objects for ordinary use, but they make art objects as well; more and more the boundary between art and craft is disappearing. In pottery, in weaving and spinning, in metalwork, the maturity, range, and sheer vitality and quality are remarkable. In woodturning and in leatherwork (which has until recently languished inexplicably in a country that produces so much raw material) there is real progress. There begins to be some very good furniture making too, as well as thatching and musical instrument making.

I believe that artists (and in that word I include our present craftspeople) first invent the future and then they announce it. The present great upsurge in the crafts portends a major change for the better in Irish culture. To explain why this is so, it is worth looking at the past imbalances. It is widely acknowledged that the verbal arts (writing and theater) are remarkable in Ireland, and folk music and dancing are remarkable too. It was said, with more truth than the speakers often knew, that the Irish used words in a way that was magic. But the point about magic, whether of American Indian shamans or of Irish poets, is that it is an attempt to change reality without working, to change, not external reality, but man's internal perception of that reality. In its most extreme form, in the Ghost Dance of Plains Indians, it is an attempt to obliterate present defeat and reinstate a previous golden age.

For hundreds of years the Irish experience has been one of defeat. To the indigenous Irish it seemed that people who were undeniably technologically superior, and by whom their own culture was being destroyed, were morally and culturally inferior. So we retreated into those parts of art which were portable, which needed no capital, which were strong on the past and on altering consciousness, like dancing and singing and storytelling, and we forsook those arts and skills that needed some wealth, some control of one's own life, some mastery of the physical environment, such as architecture, sculpture, painting, and all the crafts and homemaker's skills, including cooking. Art was for anesthesia, and not for building a better life. And, as everywhere in the world over the last century or so, it was assumed that the depth of one's culture was intimately related to the depth of one's pocket.

The political paroxysm that resulted in the establishment of an independent Irish state left us exhausted for the ensuing three or four decades. We had freedom in a political sense, but in a cultural and social, and even in an industrial, sense we did not know what we wanted to do with it. And now, within the last twenty years, we are beginning to know. We are beginning to find a voice, not just in poems and songs, but in pots, in weaving, in all sorts of craft objects. The artists are announcing a new phase in the repossession of our heritage.

Of course there are false starts and aesthetic problems. How does one incorporate the extraordinary legacy in material culture of Celtic Ireland? Or, at the other extreme, how does one overcome the tradition of round towers, wolfhounds, broken harps, shamrocks and leprechauns? We are not yet certain. But the seeking and the vitality are extraordinary in the work of Irish artists/craftsmen, and an authentic voice, an authentic set of styles, is emerging.

Everywhere in the world people are seeking a therapy for alienation. Ethnic "roots," ethnic cuisine and dress are part of this, but the most important part is the development of a life-style in each place—houses and house contents, cuisine, and clothing, as well as objects which reflect that place and that time and that unique local history, and which bear the mark of a particular human hand on a particular day.

Irish artists/craftsmen are announcing two things: That it is possible to overcome alienation and that it is possible to build a human and humane life, in scale and content, is a message for the whole world. And a message for us—which others may thrill to, in viewing it—that defeat and retreat are over. We are coming into possession of our birthright and are adding to a word culture, which the world acknowledges as remarkable, a material culture, a crafts culture no less extraordinary. It is very exciting. The best place to see it is here, in the shops in towns if nothing else is possible, but the best of all is up a boreen somewhere, out of the city, in the quiet and beautiful places where it is actually happening.

FROM FATHER TO SON FOR FIVE MILLENNIA

BY PETER HARBISON

Our craft is one of the oldest in the world. Our handi-
work is seen everywhere, in town, country and
village. The men who have gone before us have left
us a heritage to be proud of, and we feel our own
contribution has been for the good.

SEAMUS MURPHY, in the Preface to *Stone Mad* (1966)

O f all the carvers who have chiseled stone in Ireland through the centuries, Seamus
Murphy (1907–1975) is perhaps the only one who has gone beyond self-expression
in stone, and he left us a written account of his craft and of those who practiced it
with him. This was in *Stone Mad*, a charming book with a modest and totally disarming
eloquence that transcends his own art. Seamus Murphy was also, as it happens, one of
the most talented Irish stone carvers of this century, but—as he sadly reflects—also one of
the last. For his was a calling now answered by few, as it has been made largely redundant
by the advent of the steel-and-glass tower and the invention of the simple concrete block,
which is so ugly in comparison to a piece of stone. With a few notable exceptions—such
as Seamus Murphy, Michael Biggs, and Ken Thompson—stonemasons of the second half
of the twentieth century no longer carve beautiful inscriptions by hand; they rely instead
on unimaginative and stereotyped machine-made lettering. However, the occasional com-
mission for items such as church furniture still provides the present-day stone carver with
an opportunity of showing his artistry. Yet even as late as the beginning of this century, it
was not only tombstones, but buildings as well, that gave the stone carvers a vehicle for
expressing their inventive capabilities. It was these headstones and buildings that provided Seamus Murphy and his group of fellow craftsmen with their models which, as he

said himself, "make us realize how much of our knowledge is handed down from old times, and what small advances we have made."

Inherent in Seamus Murphy's very words is the traditional nature of stone carving, which, in Ireland, has a venerable ancestry going back literally to the Stone Age. Yet in the course of its five-thousand-year history, this tradition is not entirely unbroken, and a brief glance at its valleys as well as its peaks will make us appreciate that it was a craft which was not always just handed down from father to son for five millennia, but one which occasionally had to be reactivated and learned again, virtually from scratch.

When carving makes its first known Irish appearance on the Stone Age passage graves of County Meath, including Loughcrew, it is already a polished craft. It has no indigenous antecedents, but while there is as yet no compelling evidence to show that those who carved the designs on the passage graves about 3000 B.C. were anything but Irish, it is quite probable that the inspiration for the motifs they used may have come from overseas. Curiously, these motifs are almost always geometrical: spirals, diamond shapes, zigzags, triangles, though occasionally one can make out a very stylized human figure or face. This same love of geometrical ornament, and this same desire to reproduce the human figure—not in all its natural solidity, as the Greeks and Romans did, but in a very stylized form—are also characteristic of Celtic art at a later period, without there being any obvious connecting link in stone. For this precocious Stone Age flowering wilted early. It may have just survived into the beginning of the Bronze Age, around 2000 B.C., when we find small, circular motifs on flat stones. But after that, tomb building literally went underground, and for the remainder of the Bronze Age, a period of about fifteen hundred years, we look in vain for traces of the stone carver's craft. Yet during this same long period, geometrical designs continued to be executed on gold and bronze. It is perhaps these—and long-lost woodwork—that provide the tenuous link between the love of abstract ornament and the products of the stone carver's art when they next make their appearance during the Iron Age, around 300 B.C. But here the designs, though geometric, are very different in character: the wonderfully fluid curvilinear motifs of the Celts, which had been introduced into Ireland from Central Europe. In the Iron Age, however, the stone carvers were applying their skills not to large structures such as the passage graves of the Stone Age, but rather to stones that have an existence totally independent of buildings, such as that at Turoe in County Galway, which probably had a ritual significance, as the Stone Age carvings doubtless also did. Some human heads or figures, as found, for instance, on Boa Island in County Fermanagh, may also date from the Iron Age, inspired perhaps by the three-dimensional naturalistic carvings of the Romans. But Iron Age stone carving is too scarce and too scattered for us to be able to talk of any strong tradition of stone carving in Ireland at that time, and another thousand years were to elapse before the chisel was once more applied imaginatively to stone, this time under Christian influence.

But Christianity had been established for almost three hundred years in Ireland before the stone carver was put to work in its employ. It is on cross-decorated tombstones of the kind found at Clonmacnoise that we can feel the first tentative revival of the stone carver's craft under Christian influence, and this was soon to lead to some of the greatest masterpieces of that art on Irish soil—the great high crosses of about the ninth century A.D. Those at Ahenny in County Tipperary show the carver most at home with the old curvilinear designs that Ireland had known since the misty days of its Celtic origins, and he spreads his flowing curves and spirals over the surface of the stone like the gossamer of a spider's web.

But other high crosses, at Durrow and elsewhere, introduce an innovation in the use of naturalistic figures in high relief on stonework that is monumental in every sense. If the Irish artist's innate instincts had led him since the Stone Age to reproduce the human figure in stylized form, the pressure on him must have been very strong and successful to make him turn around and produce the very antithesis of his own traditional feelings in carving naturalistic human figures in scenes illustrating the Old and New Testaments, which are such a marked characteristic of most of the major crosses. The models used by the carvers of the Irish high crosses for their figured scenes must have been introduced from abroad, yet the crosses known from a slightly earlier period in Britain are sufficiently different in style to reject any suggestion that the artists who carved the Irish crosses may have been imported from England.

It was probably not until the twelfth century that the two separate stone strands in Ireland—carving and building—were reunited again since they had last met on the Stone Age tombs. But now the marriage was here to stay, and the application of carving to stone buildings, in other words architectural sculpture, was to remain a common feature in Ireland right down to our own century. The Christian combination of these two elements in twelfth-century Ireland was a particularly felicitous one. The round-headed doorways, chancel arches, and occasionally the windows of churches in the Romanesque style were decorated with an interestingly Irish admixture of geometrical ornaments and human heads. The style had been developed a century earlier in Continental Europe, but its arrival in Ireland led on from Cormac's Chapel in Cashel to some of the small Romanesque churches, such as Mona Incha in County Tipperary, or the Nuns' Church in Clonmacnoise. The development continued through Clonfert Cathedral to some of the hauntingly beautiful abbeys of the early thirteenth century in the west of Ireland, of which Ballintubber and Cong are among the finest examples.

But while this native variant of the Romanesque style was running its course in Connacht, developments were taking place in the eastern half of the country that were to alter radically the style of building—and of the carvings which adorned them. The Cistercians were the first of the Continental religious orders to establish a monastery in Ireland—at Mellifont in 1142. Their founder, Saint Bernard of Clairvaux, had railed against the use of distracting grotesque sculptures of the kind found on Romanesque structures, and the earliest Cistercian churches in Ireland were sparing in their use of decoration. The French brought their own masons with them to build Mellifont. But by the time some of the western abbeys of the order came to be built—Boyle in Roscommon or Corcomroe in Clare—the Irish builders probably felt themselves sufficiently far removed from Saint Bernard's strictures to apply boldly carved ornament more liberally.

The other important event in the east of Ireland in the twelfth century was the advent of the Normans from Britain. They joined with the newly arrived religious orders to spread their Gothic style of architecture, characterized by the pointed arch, which remained dominant until the sixteenth century. It is in some of the cathedrals erected by the Normans in Ireland in the late twelfth and thirteenth centuries that we find the first clear indications of the introduction of stone carvers from the west of England who created capitals of heads in foliage and other ornamentation. But most of the tombs in which these Normans were buried, surrounded by effigies of themselves as knights in their battle attire, were probably carved by local craftsmen in Norman employ.

The Black Death, that dreadful plague which struck terror throughout Europe from 1347 until 1352, tolled the death knell of early Norman sculpture in Ireland. It was the Gaelic parts of Ireland in the West, which suffered much less from the devastations of the plague, that were among the first to recover. The new spate of Franciscan friaries built there in the first half of the fifteenth century heralded the revival of church building, with the concomitant addition of stone carving. Throughout the second half of the century, and on into the sixteenth, Ireland experienced a feverish building activity, which gave Irish stone carvers new opportunities to express their talents in architectural and funerary sculpture, and we find whole families of carvers, such as the O'Tunneys in Kilkenny, active in the period. But the dissolution of the monasteries by Henry VIII removed many of the patrons, whom the carvers so badly needed, and their art went into a long and gradual decline in quality.

During the seventeenth century, stone carvers still had their moments. We find tombs at Lorrha and Killinaboy decorated with sensitive floral ornament in very light relief and others bearing the instruments of the Passion. In Meath there is an interesting series of wayside commemorative crosses erected by the ladies of the Bathe family. But the buildings of this turbulent period gave stone carvers, as opposed to masons (though the two at times may have been the same), little chance of artistic expression.

During the eighteenth century, most of the native population were so poor and downtrodden that they could scarcely afford tombstones, though visits to country churchyards reveal a series of exquisite gravestones of the period, carved in the lightest of relief and bearing gracefully shaped lettering. At the same time, the new Ascendancy landowners busied themselves with the construction of great mansions in the Georgian style, and until the Act of Union in 1801, Irish carvers were able to play an important role in their adornment by the production of sculptures in the Classical style and of a remarkably high quality. Also forthcoming were commissions for tombs showing their owners in an elegantly reclining pose.

Even before Emancipation came in 1829, the Catholic Church was beginning to build the myriad of parish churches that so dominated the Irish landscape in the nineteenth century, their spires taller than those of the Protestants', and their style a Neo-Gothic to suggest an unbroken link with the days before the Reformation. But in many cases the money available only allowed the building of the church, not its sculptural ornamentation, as the number of uncarved bosses on these churches confirms.

It was not until the second half of the last century that stone carvers began to come into their own in the general ornamentation of buildings, particularly in the floral capitals that are so much a feature of the period. But it was not only on churches that they practiced their art. Commercial buildings, particularly banks and even railway stations, gave great scope. Some of the stone carvers, such as C.W. Harrison and Padraic Pearse's father, came from England. But the best known of them, the O'Shea brothers, came—like Seamus Murphy—from Cork. They were prodigious workers who utilized the freedom of design advocated by John Ruskin. It is said of the O'Sheas that they would go out into the meadows in the morning and pick a bunch of flowers, which they would then arrange artistically on their workbenches and, by the close of the day, they would have carved them in stone for a capital of the Museum Building in Trinity College, Dublin, designed by Benjamin Woodward according to Ruskin's dictates.

This great floruit of the stone carver, which has left such a significant mark on the nineteenth-century buildings of Ireland, lasted just into our own century. But its gradual decline was accelerated by the design of buildings which largely eschewed carving and, as pointed out already, the advent of the concrete block dealt a death blow from which architectural sculpture is unlikely to recover. But while it is sad to reflect on the virtual disappearance of a trade that has a history longer than practically any other in Ireland, it is salutary to realize just how much it has added to the buildings and monuments that have survived down to our own day, and that form a heritage of which the country can be justly proud. What would Ireland be without its decorated passage graves, its high crosses, its medieval churches, its Georgian buildings, and its array of nineteenth-century structures, not to mention a millennium of tombstones? What frequently gives them their particular quality and interest is the art of the Irish stone carver, who was often stimulated to give of his best by using designs, sometimes of native, but often of foreign, origin, which he adapted to suit his own individual mode of expression. We may not experience much of his ingenuity in the future, but we cannot help being reminded of his craft no matter where we move in Ireland, for men like Seamus Murphy and his artistic forebears have greatly enriched our country's heritage. But even where carving is not involved, Irish artistry in stone can still enchant, and nowhere is that expressed in more simple yet lasting form than in one of the most traditional of all Irish types of stone work, the stone wall, which gives the landscape of the west of Ireland so much of its character by knitting together its patchwork of fields into an irregular but harmonious whole.

PAGE 161 *Escort for King Puck, Puck Fair, Killorglin, County Kerry*

ABOVE *Grandfather and granddaughter, the annual Bansha Show, County Tipperary*

BELOW *Traditional musicians, Clifden, County Galway*

ABOVE   *At the annual Horse Fair, Ballinasloe, County Galway*

BELOW   *The annual Bansha Show, County Tipperary*

ABOVE *Parade celebrating Puck Fair, Killorglin, County Kerry*

OPPOSITE, ABOVE *Wren-boys at Listowel, County Kerry, harvest festival*

OPPOSITE, BELOW *At the Phoenix Park races, Dublin*

PAGES 166 AND 167   *Horse Fair, Ballinasloe, County Galway*

ABOVE   *Hounds of the famous Galway Blazers, at the Dublin Horse Show*

OPPOSITE   *Louth Hunt in progress, Drogheda*

Gaelic football: All-Ireland Final, Croke Park, Dublin

Hurling was played in Ireland in pre-Christian times.
It is the fastest field game in the world.

ONCE THROUGH TARA'S HALLS

BY CIARÁN MACMATHÚNA

In 1792 a significant but sad gathering of harpers took place in Belfast; sad because this was almost the swan song of the "harp that once through Tara's halls the soul of music shed"; significant because this gathering was the source of the great Edward Bunting collection, *The Ancient Music of Ireland*.

In his description of Ireland (*Topographia Hibernica*), back in the twelfth century, Giraldus Cambrensis said that the Irish harpers were the best he had heard in all his travels. Praise indeed coming from this much-traveled ecclesiastic, because the same learned gentleman had little else that was good to say about us.

The harpers of old were not folk musicians; they were a professional body who went through a strict schooling and played for a select audience. Their patrons were the heads or chiefs of the old Irish ruling families and later the Anglo–Irish gentry. The most celebrated harper-composer about whose life and work we know a great deal was Turlough O'Carolan (1670–1738). O'Carolan has been called the last of the Irish bards, a rather romantic description, but to a certain extent true, when you remember that the tradition of which he was a part and which went back over a thousand years was fast coming to an end in the eighteenth century.

The MacDermott Roe family of Alderford near Ballyfarnon in County Roscommon were his principal benefactors and it was to this house that he returned to die in 1738. When O'Carolan became totally blind at the age of eighteen as a result of smallpox, Mrs. MacDermott Roe arranged for his training as a harper and supplied him with money, a servant, and a horse. Wherever he went he was received as a welcome guest, not as a hired musician. In return, he wrote and played music for his hosts and composed songs in the Irish language praising their families and their hospitality.

Our own day has seen a welcome revival of interest in O'Carolan due to the research of Donal O'Sullivan and the work of Gráinne Yeats, Sean O'Riada, Derek Bell, and the Chieftains, who introduced O'Carolan's music to a wide new audience.

Wolfe Tone went along to the Harp Festival in Belfast in July 1792 but wasn't impressed. "Strum, strum and be hanged. . . . no new musical discovery; believe all the good Irish airs are already written." How wrong he was! While O'Carolan and all the harpers before him and to a lesser degree after him were "strumming" for the big houses, the ordinary people of the countryside were playing their own music and singing their own songs. This was the "Hidden Ireland" and the heritage of Gaelic folk song was its soul.

It is an unaccompanied form of singing, not relying on the rhythms or the harmony of conventional Western music; an art that allows the individual traditional voice to decorate the basic melody with improvised ornamentation.

The repertoire was as wide as human experience, and people sang about most of the things that have concerned men and women since speech was heightened into song. They expressed their longing for the return of Prince Charlie and the Stuart dynasty. They sang impossible promises to children to coax them to sleep; they sang about God and life and death; about whiskey (*uisce beathadh*), the water of life; they sang about places to which they were passionately attached and lamented the destruction of familiar landscape.

> Cad a dheanfaimíd feasta gan adhmad;
> Tá deireadh na gcoillte ar lár;
> Níl trácht ar Chill Chais ná a teaghlach;
> Is ní cluinfear a cling go brách.

> (What will we do henceforth for timber;
> The last of the woods are down;
> Kilcash and its household are forgotten;
> And its bells will not be heard ever again.)

The most considerable body of Gaelic folk song is about love and more often than not about unrequited love; and the crying voice is usually of the girl who has been deserted or betrayed. These are delicate lyrical outpourings of a broken heart and not narrative ballads. With their intensity and sincerity of feeling and exquisite imagery, wedded to haunting, elusive melodies, they must take their place with the great folk songs of the world.

But the song cannot be isolated from the singer; both must go together to give the complete aesthetic and emotional effect. It was a deeply moving experience to hear the late Caitlín Maude sing of the poor girl who has been deserted by her young lover, Dónal Óg.

> Tá mo chroí-se brúite briste,
> Mar bheadh leac oighre ar uachtar uisce.

(My heart is crushed and broken,
like the ice on top of the water.)

Bhain tú an ghealach agus bhain tú an ghrian dhíom;
Agus is ro-mhor m'fhaitíos gur bhain tú Dia dhíom.
(You took the moon from me and you took the sun;
And I am very much afraid that you have deprived me of God Himself.)

As the English language spread throughout the country, replacing in whole or in part the older Gaelic tradition, songs in the new language began to increase and multiply. Some of these were imports and included versions of English and Scottish ballads that told of kings and queens and the tragedies of lords and ladies:

The rain falls on my heavy locks and the dew wets my skin;
The babe is cold in my arms, O, Lord Gregory, let me in;
Lord Gregory is not here and henceforth can't be seen;
For he's gone to bonnie Scotland to bring home his new Queen.

Many of the English songs were lyrics, perhaps not of the same intensity as their Gaelic counterparts, though sometimes dressed in Gaelic clothes and retaining the internal rhymes of Gaelic verse:

Of late I'm captivated by a handsome young man,
and I'm daily complaining for my own darling John.

Generally speaking, the songs in English were narrative ballads telling of local, national, and even international events. Hundreds of them found their way on to crudely printed ballad sheets, adorned with quaint woodcuts, and sold at fairs and other public gatherings. On these sheets Napoleon, Robert Emmet, and the great Liberator, Daniel O'Connell, had to rub shoulders with convicted murderers, Limerick rakes, and cruel landlords.

Sporting events brought out the best in the balladeers and the Sporting Races of Galway produced one immortal verse that has an ecumenical lesson for our own time:

There was half a million people there of all denominations,
The Catholic, the Protestant, the Jew and Presbyterian,
There was yet no animosity no matter what persuasion,
But failte [welcome] and hospitality inducing fresh acquaintance.

Emigration and exile, particularly to America, were an endless source of inspiration and allowed the local poet to indulge the very old Irish, almost sensuous, fascination with place names, even foreign ones:

I've travelled through Columbia's shores, all toils and dangers scorning,
To the farthest eastern border and westward to the deep;
The broad extended cotton fields and plains of Alabama;
The mines of lone Montana and the Rockies wild and steep.

But have we no place in this traditional world for the popular concert songs of the nineteenth century? Have we no consideration or consolation for the good people who believed that Moore's *Melodies* were the authentic voice of Ireland? Thomas Moore (1779–1852) did indeed use old Irish airs, had them adapted for his own purposes, and wrote for them exquisite verses that delighted the drawing rooms and salons of Dublin and London.

At the beginning of this century a more virile, national feeling, based on the new literary and Gaelic revival, was inclined to reject Moore but, of course, even in his own life his *Irish Melodies* had been dismissed by William Hazlitt in one of the cleverest and most devastating pieces of criticism ever written: "Mr. Moore converts the wild harp of Erin into a musical snuff-box." Moore, however, needs no apologia from us. "The Meeting of the Waters," "The Last Rose of Summer," and all the other songs will survive no matter what we say. We can apply to Moore what Colm Ó Lochlainn wrote about another song writer, Francis A. Fahy (1856–1935), who gave us "The Queen of Connemara" and "The Ould Plaid Shawl": "His songs have cheered many an exile, brought tears to longing eyes, and guided many a wanderer home."

The most obvious manifestation of the strength and vitality of Irish traditional music today is to be found in the instrumental music. Never before have been heard so many pipes, fiddles, flutes, tin whistles, accordions, concertinas, banjos and *bodhráns* (a traditional tambourine, pronounced *bow-rawn*, and generally made from goatskin).

The uileann pipes are the most distinctive of these. *Uileann* is the Gaelic word for *elbow*; the air for the instrument is generated not through a mouthpiece, as in the warpipes, but by means of a bellows tied to one elbow.

Even though slow airs or song tunes are played on the various instruments, the most popular repertoire is dance music: reels, jigs, hornpipes, and polkas. But the music is not the servant of the dance and is generally played and listened to for its own sake, without the intrusion of dancers. This is not to devalue the importance of traditional dances, which are still very much part of the entertainment of the Irish countryside, particularly the country sets, which are group dances for young and old with no special costumes. These must be distinguished from the more formal, competitive, yet very popular, schools of Irish dancing that cater to hundreds of young athletic, costumed pupils, "gorgeous and caparisoned from head to heel in all kinds of sartorial splendour," as Canon Sheehan said about the Yank in *Glenanaar*.

Over the last thirty years or so Irish traditional music has come out into the open, out from the country kitchen and city back rooms and attracted to itself huge audiences at home and abroad. The reasons for this phenomenal revival or reawakening of interest are complex, but the contribution of organizations like Comhaltas Ceoltóirí Éireann (the association of Irish traditional musicians), the Oireachtas Gaelic Festival and the national broadcasting station, Radio Telefis Éireann, must be acknowledged.

Certain individuals also created a new enthusiasm and new audience for the old music. Sean O'Riada (1931–1971) in his short life, and in an almost charismatic way, gave an awareness of the Irish musical heritage to a generation that had ignored it or knew nothing about it. This O'Riada did in the 1960s with his Ceoltóirí Cualann group of traditional musicians and through his music for the historical documentary film *Mise Éire* and through his Gaelic Mass. Out of this movement came one of our most popular groups, the Chieftains, who have brought Irish traditional music westward to the Golden Gate of San Francisco and eastward to the Great Wall of China.

Irish traditional music has never been so popular, but where this popularity will lead is an open question. We can only hope that the music will never become too standardized but will retain its regional and local character, and that musicians will play and still have an audience in their own communities.

GREGARIOUS, LOQUACIOUS, AND ADDICTED TO CELEBRATION

BY BRYAN MACMAHON

God has made the Irish gregarious, loquacious, and addicted to celebration. The celebration, whether by way of feast, fair, or festival, may be either secular or devotional. Or, indeed, a traditional mixture of both.

The Irish fair has roots that go deep into the history, parahistory, and legend of the Celtic people. The assembly, or fair, held at Tailteann in County Meath over two thousand years ago, at which the High King of Tara presided and at which all quarrels and disputes were rigidly prohibited, could well have had its still more remote origin in games associated with funeral rites.

As a sideshow to the games held in conjunction with this fair, young men selected their brides by the choice of a shapely arm appearing through an aperture in a rock face. The union, if deemed unsuitable, could be dissolved after a year and a day. The ceremony of severance was brief: The young man and young woman stood on a nearby hill; one faced north, the other south, and on a given signal they stalked away from each other.

Medieval fairs at which farm animals were bought and sold originated in charters granted by the English crown. Naturally, these monarchs liked to keep a check on Irish assemblies. Many of these fairs are still held and may have local names: The Gooseberry Fair, held, say, when gooseberries are ripe; the Fair of Spancil Hill in County Clare, which is enshrined in balladry; and "The Old Lammas Fair of Ballycastle-O," held in an area replete with age-old legends, in County Antrim in the extreme north, where "dulse and yalla man"—seagrass and toffee—are resolutely chewed.

Paramount in folk annals, however, is Puck Fair, held in Killorglin, County Kerry. Here, on August 10 each year, a Puck, in the form of a royally bedecked billy goat, is paraded through thronged streets, ceremoniously crowned by a comely maiden, and then winched to a lofty throne above the host. Then for three days—the Gathering Day, the Binding, or Fair, Day, and the Scattering Day—he presides over the festivities.

So remote are the beginnings of this fair that various theories are advanced for its origin. The exalted billy goat may have been a pagan symbol of male potency; a more prosaic explanation has it that in the manner of the geese of ancient Rome, a goat gave warning of the approach of an enemy force. More acceptable still is the legend that the patent of the fair almost lapsed when no beast was offered for sale on the appointed day. However, day and patent both were preserved by an old countrywoman's most timely offering of her billy goat for sale.

Finally, His Capric Majesty having been dethroned, the tinkers, roustabouts, fruit sellers, three-card trick men, fortunetellers, and tramps, together with all the country folk from hell to bedlam, disperse to dream of yet another focus of folk activity. And this, as often as not, could be associated with the horse.

When cavalry was a force in European armies, the imminence of war could be determined by the demand for a certain type of horse at such fairs as the Great Fair of Ballinasloe in County Galway or the Fair of Cahirmee in County Cork.

One can visit Galway and from there travel west through an Irish-speaking area to Clifden, where on Show Day, or Fair Day, one could view that lovely animal of indigenous breed known as the Connemara pony. But I made my way to Cahirmee where, tradition has it, Napoleon's horse Marengo was purchased.

I noted that the horse-drawn barrel-bodied tinker-and-gypsy-type caravan was, sadly, being replaced by the motor-drawn type of living wagon. But I was able to hold a conversation in Shelta, the secret language of the Irish tinkers, with an old traveler friend. I watched the fair proper, where half-Thoroughbreds, used by such hunting packs as the Scarteens and the Kildares, were being ridden up and down by young ladies, their fawn jodhpurs, dark-green jackets, and peaked caps contrasting with the wild garb of tinker lads riding barebacked and "hooshing" their hairy ponies through the throngs.

Amidst the hullabaloo of the fair, I met an old man well into his eighties who confided to me that as a lad of eighteen he had fallen in love with an "Ascendancy lady" whom he had admired for her seat on a horse. He had first seen her in Cahirmee seventy years before, and even as we chatted, his eyes kept scanning the crowds as if to see again the damsel of his dreams.

On a more patrician level, the Dublin Horse Show, held in early August, and its brother the Spring Show of early May see the best of Irish bloodstock on parade, while in the International Teams jumping competitions the show jumper comes into his own. Gray toppers and high jinks at midnight on the part of Old Ascendancy and *nouveau riche* twin, conjoined in festivity. Both groups, however, rejoice when, from the small fields of the countryside, there arrives a heart-stopping "lepper" like Boomerang, ridden by Eddie Macken.

When it comes to racing proper, not a word will I speak against the major racetracks of the East Coast. But far closer to the bone of my-kind-of-Ireland is Galway Races, where in late July the Irish West gathers in communal celebration. Although the "Western World" of Synge has vanished, an important residue is still in evidence at Galway.

Further to the southwest, my native county of Kerry holds three Carnival Race Meetings. Killarney Races, held in mid-July, has a backdrop of beauty in purple peaks and the glitter of lake water; appropriately, it holds a competition to select the most fashionably dressed lady attending the event.

Twenty miles to the north, Tralee Races of late August bubbles over to become the Festival of Kerry, having as its showpiece the selection of a young woman from any part of the globe (providing she has proof of some Irish ancestry) who most closely approximates the idealized belle of beauty and grace immortalized in the song "The Rose of Tralee."

> It was not her beauty alone that won me
> Oh no, 'twas the truth in her eyes ever dawning . . .

Peripheral to Southwest Ireland's final annual fling, Listowel Harvest Festival of Racing, held in late September, an event which for a full week scorns to separate night from day, is where one may meet band after band of torchlit wren-boys, grotesquely dressed, dancing, singing, and drumming until the stars grow wan in the morning sky.

Perhaps the most enjoyable of all the festivals of Ireland (All-Ireland Hurling and Gaelic Football Finals apart) are the traditional music festivals known as Fleadhanna (Irish *Fleadh*, a feast, pronounced *Flah*) which, building up from village, county, and provincial events, reach a climax in the National Fleadh Cheoil na hÉireann, again held in late August.

The town selected to host the National Fleadh must have certain characteristics. It must have a music-loving population, intimate streets with nooks suitable for impromptu open-air music sessions, a plethora of halls to house the various competitions, a park capable of holding ten to fifteen thousand campers, and a wide range of guest-houses and hotels.

Towns such as Clones, Ennis, Mullingar, Buncrana, Listowel, and latterly, Kilkenny City are favorite locations for the National Festival of Traditional Music.

As the date of the National Fleadh approaches, the cream of Irish traditional musicians, streaming in from all corners of the land and indeed from the ends of the earth, head for the chosen venue where they will compete for the Blue Riband of virtuosity in the particular section they have chosen. The flags of the Celtic nations are raised in the town park. The houses re-echo the music of flutes, fiddles, pipes, harps, concertinas, accordions, tin whistles, and xylophones. The atmosphere grows tense as in hall after hall the moment of adjudication draws near. The windowpanes rattle as, in the narrow streets outside, marching bands go by—at times under the stern batons of strutting nuns. In the pubs, over foaming tankards, grace-noted ballads of emigration and rebellion are sung, crystallizing the pathos and passion of an older Ireland.

Hitherto I have mentioned only the profane gatherings of celebration. In many villages, devotional "patterans," akin to the French *pardons*, perpetuate the memory of a local saint. Some of these festivals are associated with wells: This is understood to indicate that, over fifteen hundred years ago, Saint Patrick and his successors "sanctified" ancient pagan rites and sites.

In Ballyvourney, an Irish-speaking oasis in County Cork, Saint Gobnat is revered at Whitsun, vernacularly referred to as "the Fitchin." A dumpy little statue of Saint Gobnat, by my good friend the late Seamus Murphy, R.H.A., depicting this female saint wearing a traditional cloak and standing on a beehive, presides over the penitential and recreational exercises. In the ancient graveyard lies buried the musician Sean O'Riada, whose fine work bridged the classical and traditional musical streams of Ireland.

Close to the towering Cliffs of Moher in Clare, I recall in former days seeing the Aran Islanders come ashore from their canvas-covered curraghs at Doolin pier and, moving soundlessly on *pampooties*, a type of moccasin or primitive shoe made from raw cowhide, murmur the prayers associated with the "rounds" of Saint Brigid's Well. Through its pubs, O'Connor's and McDermott's, Doolin has won international fame as a center of traditional music.

Nor is this custom of well rites confined to the Irish South and West: in Struel, a few miles east of Downpatrick in the hard-headed North, and close to Saul, where Saint Patrick founded his first church, there are four traditional wells. One is for drinking, one for eye cures, and the remaining two for bathing. Votaries at the wells often leave behind tokens ranging from rags to coins. I can't recall where it was I once saw a golf tee, tied to a bush above one of these wells.

North beyond the Twelve Pins, or Bens, of Connemara—an area rich in dedication to local saints and close to Westport in County Mayo—is Croagh Patrick, where fifteen hundred years ago Saint Patrick fasted and prayed for forty days. Here, on the last Sunday in July each year, tens of thousands of pilgrims stumble through the darkness on the jagged mountainside. They hear Mass on the summit in the gray dawn with the minor archipelago of Clew Bay fitfully visible through the mist below.

Still further north in County Donegal, in what is called Saint Patrick's Purgatory, a basilica seems to rise out of the dark water of Lough Derg and is reached by a black boat reminiscent of Charon's Stygian vessel. Here each year, pilgrims, again by the tens of thousands (by and large a happy throng) arrive to stumble sleepless and barefooted over jagged rocks and to exist on a diet of brackish tea and dark bread to atone for faults.

At Skellig Michael off the Kerry coast, on the summit of an awesome crag, lie the remains of a Celtic monastery. Here in early medieval times penitents performed dizzy feats of climbing in expiation of their sins. Gannets dive from the heights and puffins trot comically about one's boots, where once was held a pilgrimage that was condemned by the pope because of the severity of its rites. Only a tenuous thread in the form of a children's street game now reminds one of the crowded past: in Kerry towns on Shrove Tuesday evening, children armed with ropes still mime the hustling of bachelors off to Skelligs Rock, where a time lag in the church calendar once allowed laggard lovers to marry during a forbidden period in the ecclesiastical year.

Among the many kinds of Irish gatherings, the list of literary festivals is a long one. Brian Merriman, a down-to-earth poet who championed the cause of menless women, the great Yeats and the great Joyce, O'Carolan the harper, Patrick McGill the navvy writer, P. J. McCall the balladmaker, and a Dublin street rhymer called Zozimus of the Liberties are all publicly honored in one form or another.

There are festivals devoted to seafood and strawberries, piping and curragh racing, oysters and bachelors. The Siamsa of Tralee is a superb evocation of folk ritual, while international actor Eamon Kelly can make a festival of his own when he spreads his fingers before the firelight and begins to tell an age-old story which begins "In my father's time..."

Did someone ask the question: With all this festivity, do the Irish work at all?

My answer is this: If all the hours which industrial societies spend in commuting were totted up, the total would show far more time gone to waste than that which the Irish, most gregariously, most agreeably, most convivially, most profitably, and indeed most piously, spend in recreation by way of feast, fair, and festival.

OVERRIDING THE POLITICAL BORDER: SPORT

BY LORD KILLANIN

An Irishman can make himself very unpopular, as I learned during my presidency of the International Olympic Committee, when he claims that the first sailing across the Atlantic was by the Irish monk, Brendan the Navigator, as recorded in the medieval text *Navigatio*. The feasibility of this pre-Columbian landing on the mainland of America was proved possible by the author, archaeologist, and historian Tim Severin in his book *The Brendan Voyage*, an account of his crossing of the Atlantic in a leather boat. But if this early sailing adventure is only legendary, the fact that there were Irish games of an Olympic nature at least five hundred years before the first Olympic Games in 1370 B.C. is much more convincing. The most famous of the ancient athletic games were those known as Aonach Tailteann, the most ancient organized sport known.

These games took their name from Tailte, wife of Eochaidh MacErc, the king of Ireland in the earliest days. He had been slain in battle at Moytura by an invading colony known as the Tuatha Dé Danaan, which landed about four thousand years ago. Tailte took up her residence at the royal palace of Tara in the present County Meath, and the sites of these earliest games were on what is now Loughcrew in County Meath near the village of Teltown.

Sport in the neighboring island of Britain appears to have come with the invasion of the Normans in the eleventh century, when "the nobles for the first time devoted themselves to the chase and joust whilst people played games or ball on the village green."

In Ireland the ancient games, which frequently took place on high ground, were closely associated with the festival of Lughnasa. This festival is still celebrated in some parts of

Ireland on what is known as Garland Sunday at the end of July or the beginning of August. The rural communities went to certain heights or waterside sites to spend the day in festivities and sports, besides perhaps collecting bilberries for consumption and for preserving. This main custom was also traditional in other Celtic lands, especially the Isle of Man, Cornwall, and Wales.

The festival known in Irish as *Aonach* was a national public assembly at which kings and queens, warrior chieftains, and men of learning would meet to lay down the laws of the country, paying homage to the illustrious dead and entertaining the people with sport. At the close of the day torches were lit from the fire that had cremated the dead and, as the column of black smoke ascended from the high ground, the crowds turned their faces to the setting sun, raising their hands in salute to the departing God of the Day.

As at the Olympic Games, there was much protocol and ceremony, but, unlike the ancient Olympic Games, where a Vestal virgin was the only female witness, women were welcome as spectators and there was much matchmaking. It was a time of peace between the rival tribes and kingdoms that formed the ancient nation of Ireland. There was a strict code of ethics and behavior as there is in modern sport, and at the same time there was close contact with visitors and traders from Greece. Sports included running, throwing of quoits, and horse-and-chariot racing. Ancient Ireland was a country of sport.

This tradition has continued, with most sports overriding the political border. The indigenous Irish sports are governed by a committee of the famous Gaelic Athletic Association, which boasts over three thousand affiliated clubs and in relation to the size of our population is perhaps one of the most influential, purely amateur organizations in the world. Unfortunately its games are not widely known internationally, although in recent years the games have been seen increasingly on television and are practiced in countries to which the Irish have emigrated, such as the United States, Australia, and Britain.

The Gaelic Athletic Association was formed in 1884 by the Archbishop of Cashel, Dr. Croke. It had a nationalistic outlook, was extremely democratic, and has contributed greatly to the health and well-being of the country. The principal games are hurling, Gaelic football, Gaelic handball, and a form of rounders which is still played, especially in the North. Despite the word "Athletic" in the title, the GAA no longer includes track-and-field, although it did so from its foundation until 1921, when unfortunately there was a split from which track-and-field athletes of Ireland are still suffering, as are the cyclists.

After the foundation of the GAA, sport was no longer confined to the occupying British and the privileged classes. However, in order to ensure its purity, what became known as "garrison" games, that is, games played by the British, especially by those wearing the King's or Queen's uniform, were "banned," and no member of the GAA could play rugby, soccer, field hockey, or tennis. Happily, in April, 1971, the ban was lifted.

The All-Ireland Gaelic Football Final is the climax of the sport in the country, and every year up to ninety thousand people flock to Croke Park on the north side of Dublin to watch. Gaelic football is sometimes described as a mixture of rugby union and association football: this is because the ball may be handled but not carried, and it can be bounced for four paces. The goals, as for hurling, are similar in appearance to rugby goals in that they look like the large letter *H*, a goal, worth three points, being scored when the ball passes below the bar (not far from the height of a soccer bar) and a point being scored when the ball goes over the bar. The local club is the basis of the whole of the GAA organization, with the best players being chosen for county teams, who then compete for the championships of each province. The winning team from each province—Ulster, Munster, Leinster, and Connacht—play off until two teams remain and play in the All-Ireland Final.

Although Gaelic football is the best-attended sport in Ireland, the most exciting is hurling, which is played with a hurley, or caman, a flat ash stick, different from a field-hockey stick in that it is not rounded on one side. The ball may be carried on the stick and the stick may be raised well above the head, which it may not be in field hockey. Except perhaps for jai alai, it is the fastest team ballgame in the world, demanding great skill, courage, speed, and a very good eye. When the ball is struck by the hurley (known as a puck) it can travel over one hundred yards, so the pace up and down the field is great. I remember some years ago when Prince Rainier and Princess Grace of Monaco attended an All-Ireland Final at Croke Park the game was so fast and furious that Prince Rainier said to me, "I only hope the Latins don't learn to play this game!"

The woman's version of hurling is camogie, introduced at the turn of the century, well in advance of the emancipation of women in sport, to provide an Irish game alternative to field hockey. Physical contact is forbidden in camogie.

All ballgames, whether played with equipment (rackets or hurleys), by hand (fives or Irish handball), or with the feet or hands and only by teams (basketball and team handball), have evolved in various countries according to social, economic, and climatic conditions. Ireland has been no exception.

The handball governed by the GAA is similar to fives and is usually played on a three-sided court, although in more recent years new courts have been built with a glass back wall for the benefit of spectators. Originally like Eton fives, which were first played against the buttresses of the chapel of that school, this game must have originated from a simple country game played with the hand and a ball against the gable ends of the houses or cottages.

The GAA game of Irish rounders, played with a bat and ball and similar to American softball, is largely played in the North of Ireland. It would be possible for Irish rounders players to participate, after training, in the American game, in the same way that it has been found possible for Gaelic footballers to compete with Australia, which has developed its own football code based on rules, some of which were probably brought to Australia from Ireland.

There are also a considerable number of purely local games, one of which, road bowling, would appear to be unique to Ireland. Two players bowl a twenty-eight-ounce ball down the country lanes, roads, or boreens, and whoever has the least number of throws over an agreed distance is the winner. This game is restricted to Cork, where the players bowl overarm, and Armagh, where they bowl underarm.

Gambling in Irish sport is principally associated with racing, both horse and greyhound. Greyhound racing takes place on an enclosed track with an electric hare, the greyhounds having in many cases graduated from open coursing, in which a live hare is chased within a restricted area. This latter sport has been the subject of much controversy in recent years, but it is widely supported, especially in the province of Munster.

The center of Irish horse racing is at the Curragh (racecourse) of Kildare, which was one of the sites of the early Aonachs, or gatherings. There was racing on the Curragh three or four thousand years ago, and today it is the scene of all Irish classics, such as the Irish Derby, besides being the headquarters of the Irish Turf Club (the governing body of flat racing) and the Irish National Hunt Steeplechase Committee (the governing body of jumping racing). These two bodies control the rules and license jockeys, trainers, and racecourses. Their financing comes from subscriptions, entry fees, and charges levied on owners, trainers, jockeys and from the Government-nominated Racing Board, which controls all the finances of racing, especially the licensing of bookmakers on the tracks and the running of the totalizator. Despite the fact that there are some six thousand horses in training in Ireland, some twenty-eight courses and some million racegoers per annum, the "sport of kings" does not thrive financially as well as elsewhere. The result is that some of the racetrack facilities for the public are far from good, although the standards of horses and of grass tracks are probably the best in the world, as indeed are the stud farms. The Irish racehorse is exported worldwide and some of the best stallions stand in Ireland currently. Racing is an important industry, employing directly about fifty thousand people and indirectly many more.

The classic races are well attended, but the country people of Ireland prefer going to the National Hunt Steeplechase races. There are many Point-to-Point meetings, which Masters of the Hounds are permitted to organize. These used to be run over natural courses, with most of the horses the property of the riders or their families. In recent years the Point-to-Points have become more and more "professional," and a greater number of horses are being trained by professional trainers.

Racing is a very social sport. Although large prices are paid for good horses at sales, the approach on the racecourse is very popular and democratic. Some tracks are quite small, with a maximum attendance of two thousand people. There are holiday meetings, the most successful of which is Galway, a six-day event, and a unique meeting is held on the beach of Laytown, the day, date, and time of racing depending on the tide. There are other races on the beaches as well as in villages and towns, known as "flapper" meetings and not authorized by the official bodies.

Ireland has always played a leading role in equestrian sports as well as in racing. The climax is the Royal Dublin Society's Annual Horse Show, which takes place in early August, with the main event the Nations Cup for the Aga Khan Trophy. The Irish horse is very suitable for what is termed "Three-Day Eventing" (on the Continent, "Military" competition). This consists of a day of dressage, a day of cross country, and a day of show jumping, and it is a most grueling test for any horse. Dressage, which forms part of eventing, is a discipline of its own under the International Equestrian Federation and has only recently been taken seriously in Ireland.

Golf has long been played in Ireland, but as the interest has increased so have the number of courses, which now total over a hundred. These range from the exclusive clubs around Dublin, such as Portmarnock and Royal Dublin, to an increasing number of public courses. The principal domestic golfing event, attracting international competition, is the annual Carroll's Irish Open.

Association football (soccer) has never had quite the same attraction in Ireland as it has in Britain. This is chiefly, I believe, a matter of money, as the best teams are professional and the best players are tempted by offers from Britain and elsewhere in Europe. There are, however, semiprofessional and professional clubs throughout Ireland and after the World Cup every four years there is a very considerable increase in the number of children playing soccer. Rugby football, which originated in England in 1823 when a Rugby schoolboy picked up the ball and ran with it, has been played actively in Ireland since the middle of the nineteenth century. The Irish Rugby Football Union, an All-Ireland body, was founded in 1874, a year before the first international match against England. Ireland last won what is called "The Triple Crown" in 1982, defeating the three British unions (England, Scotland, and Wales).

Track-and-field is widely practiced. The 1932 Olympics in Los Angeles, when Bob Tisdell won the two-hundred-meter hurdle and Dr. Pat O'Callaghan the hammer Gold Medal for the second time, was the highlight in our athletic history, and we had to wait until 1956 for Ronnie Delany to win another Gold Medal for the fifteen hundred meters at Melbourne. In 1983 Eamonn Coghlan won the five thousand meters in the first World Championships at Helsinki, having been unfortunate in the Olympic Games at both Montreal and Moscow in the fifteen hundred meters.

Yachting is a natural pastime, since long seacoasts are ideal for cruising, and indeed the oldest yacht club in the world is in Cork, founded in 1720. The Irish Yachting Association administers International Yacht Racing Rules and Standards and now has taken over responsibility for board sailing (surf sailing) which was added to the program for the 1984 Los Angeles Olympics during my period as president of the International Olympic Committee. There are over a hundred yacht clubs spread around the coast of Ireland, and the South Coast in recent years has become very much a place to attract European yachtsmen. For a country with so much water it is surprising that swimming has not reached a higher standard. Here much responsibility must rest with the authorities, who have not been sufficiently aggressive regarding the building of adequate pools of Olympic size for training in swimming, diving, and water polo. Although in the last twelve years there has been a gradual improvement, standards fall well below those set by the Australians and North Americans.

The Irish have a reputation, I think unfairly, of being pugnacious. We have, however, produced many excellent boxers, some of whom have turned professional. Boxing had depended very much on the large cities, especially Belfast and Dublin, and the police forces on both sides of the border have taken an active part in the formation of youth clubs in which boxing has been a very important social factor. In 1956 at the Melbourne Olympic Games the Irish boxers won a Silver and three Bronze Medals. All the Bronze Medal winners came from Northern Ireland.

The greatest interest at the moment in Irish sport is the development of community games, which bring the young of the country together, and the government policy of sports for all, which includes sports for the handicapped. I have been connected with sport in Ireland since 1950, when I was elected president of the Olympic Council for Ireland. Unfortunately, over my years, much time has been taken up with politics rather than with the aspects of sports which interested me, such as the development of youth and competition of a nonchauvinistic nature. One thing which pleases me about sport in Ireland, however, is that despite our many differences, athletes have a common interest that transcends all boundaries.

ACKNOWLEDGMENTS

This is a joyous opportunity to thank the kind and generous people who have joined me in the adventure of this book: who encouraged, inspired, and guided me along the way.

First of all, thank you to dear friends who believed in me, which gave me the strength to persevere and turn a dream into this reality—Soren Jensen, Cheri Bottero, Joannie Roulac, Ginnie Finlay, Vivian McAteer, Chris & Fran Stritzinger, Betsy Brawley, Linus & Pat Maurer, Betty Crosby, Bobbie Stone, Owen Stebbins, Helen Nelson, Don Warning, Jane Walsh Bracha, Joe, Mindy & Maddie Warning, Debbie Kurtz, Declan Collins, Suzanne Coe, Kay French, Bill & Elisabeth Vincent, Jack & Janet O'Loughlin, Eddie Burroughs, Jack Fogarty, Monica Conway, Cathy McDermott, Barbara Sullivan, Carol Taylor, Sharon Pair-Taylor, Bill Thetford, Pat Hopkins, Jerry Jampolsky, Patsy Robinson, Ruth Crawford, Florence Yach, Hugh Richardson.

Thank you to Patricia Tunison Preston for introducing me to Ireland; Tom Kennedy, Dick Murphy, Doris Vriezen, Mary Clark, Marie Wilson, Winnie Hayes, and Pat Hanrahan for their continuous support and TLC; Bruce Michel, Pegg Nadler, Bobbie Mark and Bob Morton for leading me successfully through the publishing maze.

Thank you to my new friends in Ireland, who helped me put the pieces together and showed me Ireland through their lives—Nicholas & Julie Ann Anley, Patricia Barry, Alice Best, Tadhg & Ursula de Brun, Eamonn Burgess, Paul Dancklefsen, Paddy Derivan, Pat Dooley, Kay Dunlop, Helen O'Kane Farrelly, Jim & Avila Fitzgerald, David Fitzgibbon, Richard & Susan Filgate, Joe Flanagan, Peig Fogarty, Alan Glynn, Mamie & Davy Gunn, Bobby & Veronica Harris, Judy Hayes, Elizabeth Healy, Edmund Hourican ,Walter Kavanagh, James Larkin, Geoffrey Martin, Peter Matson, Bill Maxwell, Marcelle Moody, Tony & Angela Muckley, Jim & Kate Nicholson, Mary Prendergast, Jean Rylands, Bruce Savage, Vincent Tobin, Dick Troy, Paddy Tutty, Michael & Phyllis Vaughan.

Special thanks to James Plunkett and Bernard Share for their patience and guidance; and to all the wonderful, talented writers for their participation and friendship.

Finally, thank you to all the delightful people in Ireland who opened their hearts and homes, extended their warm hospitality, offered words of wisdom and friendship; and thanks to Ireland for teaching me about myself; there is peace beneath the conflict.

Kathleen Jo Ryan

PROJECT DIRECTOR: ROBERT MORTON
EDITOR: TERESA EGAN
DESIGNER: JUDITH HENRY

Library of Congress Cataloging-in-Publication Data
Irish traditions / edited by Kathleen Jo Ryan & Bernard Share ;
photographs by Kathleen Jo Ryan ; with essays by Cyril Cusack . . . [et al.].
p.   cm.
ISBN 0-8109-8096-7
1. Ireland—Civilization. 2. Ireland—Social life and customs. I. Ryan, Kathleen, 1943–   . II. Share, Bernard.
III. Cusack, Cyril, 1910–
[DA925.I748   1990]   941.5—dc20   89-28053   CIP

Abradale Press
Harry N. Abrams, Inc.
100 Fifth Avenue
New York, N.Y. 10011